Voyage to the Other Side of Grief

To Diane,

Grieve well!

Glenora Doherty

Voyage To The Other Side Of Grief

Voyage to the Other Side of Grief

Finding Joy in New Dreams

Glenora Doherty

First Published in Canada 2011 by Life Journey Publishing (Imprint of Influence Publishing)

Front cover artwork & design: Tara Dong

Praise

Glenora is a woman of great strength and unquenchable joy. Her story is one of great love, great loss, and great faith. I'm confident that those dealing with loss will also find hope on the other side of grief as they read her story.
Ian Lopez, Pastor, New Beginnings Community Church. Surrey, BC

Glenora shares her journey of grief through poignant memories and delightful adventures, broken dreams and new beginnings, pitfalls and surprising blessings… It is rich in detail and insights from her own experience. You will cry. You will laugh. You will learn about "stages of grief", helpful "steps to survival", yet also how every grief journey is unique.
Irene Flett, Co-Director, Coastal Counselling Services, Surrey, BC

Losing your Captain as a result of an accident at sea or illness is one of those things all cruising couples fear. It's easy to get caught up in the day-to-day joy of cruising and ignore the realities of life, but Glenora reminds us how important it is to plan ahead for such an eventuality. I cried when I read this book, but I also laughed when she related some of her cruising stories and I certainly loved sharing those happy joyful moments with her by remembering my own cruising days. This is a book every sailor should read!
Julie Salisbury, Author of "A Seven Year Journey around the World - Discovering my Passion and Purpose"

Peter Ronald Douglas Doherty, 1943-2005

To Peter

Voyage To The Other Side Of Grief

Acknowledgements

My first thanks go to my family with love – my son Ryan and his wife Jackie, my daughter Tara and her husband Brian, and my five adorable grandchildren: Angie, Daryan, Trea, T'ea and Matthew. You have always just been there for me. The fact that Ryan and his family returned from Peru to live in Canada within months of my husband's death is one of God's greatest blessings. And grateful thanks to my incredibly talented and creative daughter, Tara, for designing and producing the beautiful artwork on the cover of this book and creating my W5 Communications logo. Thank you also for guiding me through the world of social media and website design. We three (Ryan, Tara and I) have helped each other and our entire family settle into a new life – one that still holds a very big empty space. However, it's a good life and gets more rewarding every day as we grow stronger together and as my grandchildren get more beautiful and develop their own unique talents. I can't begin to list everything each one of you has done for me on this voyage, but you're part of my story; your names are mentioned in nearly every chapter of this book. Your Dad and Poppa loved you so much and would be so proud of you today if he were here! Thanks also to my S-I-L Jennifer, who came soon after her brother's death to cook, clean and do everything necessary to care for the rest of us, to assist in the preparations for the Peter's Celebration of Life Service, and to share her advice about grieving with me. She was still grieving for the loss of her other brother.

Thank you to all my long-time Bluewater Cruising Association (BCA) friends: David and Carol Smith, who helped check out *Wanderlust V*'s engine when I returned to Mazatlan, volunteered to crew with me to get *Wanderlust V* across the Sea of Cortes to La Paz, and later helped me identify and place a value on the carloads of spare parts that came off the boat. Likewise, Jackie and Manfred

Melzer also helped me sort through spare parts, equipment and garbage on the boat, and helped load it up to go to swap meets, consignment stores or the dump! Sally Holland was there to greet *Wanderlust V* in Ladner in 2006, hosted a welcome home dinner, and has given me much advice based on her own experience as a widow. With her years of experience as co-editor and copy editor of BCA's monthly newsletter, *Currents,* so she was the first person I asked to proofread this book. Several Past Commodores of BCA encouraged, supported and inspired me in many ways: Blake Williams capably acted as MC for the reception following Peter's service and then rounded up a group of talented musicians for the Irish Wake that evening; Perry Boeker spoke so well in the service about Peter's cruising life and contributions to BCA; and Don Brown was the one who saw my own leadership abilities and launched me on the BCA executive path. He also shares a beautiful spiritual story in this book in Chapter 6. And a special thank you to fellow sailors and authors, Anne Brevig and Catherine Dook, for reviewing and recommending this book to others, and for all the information and support you have given me throughout the publishing process. And most of all, I thank my friends and former boat neighbours Barb Angel and Ian Monsarrat for everything they have done for me and Peter for many years before Peter's death and ever since. They are mentioned frequently in this book. And the wonderful thing is that I still have all these friends today - they are a big part of my life.

Words cannot describe how much I learned and gained from New Beginnings Community Church. This caring, loving congregation taught me the value of being part of a community of believers in a patient and non-judgemental way - and brought me back to faith. They provided physical support too - meals and transportation for weeks after Peter's death, then used furniture, toys and household items to furnish a suite for my son and his family. Other members of this church have given special gifts: Karen Perinbam and Doug Collins of Steppin' Out Productions created the CD of Peter's piano music that was given to everyone who attended Peter's service; Debbie Judas and Beth Turner were the first friends to come to the hospital after Peter's death to pray with Tara and me, and continue to be a part of my life. Thank you, Beth for graciously relinquishing your claim on the basement suite so I could live there, and for connecting me with my publisher. And Debbie – I have watched you grow as a pastor and facilitator of spiritual retreats and I admire and thank you for all the clarity and peace you've given me. I've loved joining you for coffee and conversation - and your "girls nights" rock! However, most of my thanks to New Beginnings go to my incredible Pastor, Ian Lopez. Your own down-to-earth faith is an inspiration to me, as were your stimulating sermons and wonderful music. You've made me laugh, cry and think. Thank you also for reviewing this book for me. And to Ian's Mom, my newest best friend forever, Netty Lopez. I give thanks for the friendship we've developed – one that would never have happened if Peter were still alive today because I wouldn't have had the opportunity to meet you. Thank you all for welcoming me as part of your community, becoming part of my life and bringing me back to a closer relationship with our God.

Thanks also go to all the counsellors, medical staff, social workers, and organizations that helped me grieve: Irene Flett (who wrote the Foreword to this book), my family doctor, Mike Myckatyn, and the Surrey Hospice Society where I learned so much about grieving, not only with others, in a grief therapy group, but from their library.

Then there are long-time friends that I met at RCAF Stn 3 Wing, Zweibruecken, Germany, over 40 years ago – especially Ken and Penny Carpenter. Penny was beside me within 24 hours of Peter's death, Ken arrived and spoke at Peter's service about his military career. He has become Uncle Ken to my son, Ryan, a father replacement if you will. Ken was there to help walk me through the maze of paperwork and estate matters after Peter's death, and I extend heartfelt thanks to my dear friend Penny, a talented artist who contributed the two pen and ink sketches that appear as illustrations in this book. Even before Peter's death, she was Momma Penny to my daughter, when I was off sailing in Mexico. And it was just after Peter's death that Penny and Ken introduced me to Claudia Guichon, to whom I am also grateful. She patiently taught me, a sailor with thousands of ocean miles, how to swim - which enabled me to discover new dreams and joys.

My thanks go also to the Maple Leaf Singers, and our incredible director, Wilson Fowlie. It's a group that allowed me to enjoy a new dream – singing in a mixed chorus once again. No matter what stresses I have during the day, going to an evening rehearsal and singing with all of you makes me smile and restores my joy in life.

How grateful I am that I found Dennison Berwick to be my editor! Through his comments, suggestions and corrections, he has taught me so much about editing and writing a book. Having spent the majority of my professional career as an editor (of correspondence, briefing notes, articles, reports, etc.) I thought I knew a lot about editing. Was I ever in for a big surprise! I discovered it's a whole new ball game. As a sailor himself, he was also able to give me advice about how technical my nautical vocabulary should be in this book. And finally, to my publisher, Julie Salisbury, for her passion to inspire others to write. She's also a sailor, and so she truly understood my loss. I always wanted to write a book and have years of handwritten journals and printed short stories and articles stowed away, but didn't know how to begin to put it all together. She showed me how, through her InspireABook workshop, the simplest book building system in the world. I couldn't have done it without her encouragement, experience and bubbly laugh. And thank you to all the other authors who are part of Julie's author circles, for your encouragement, advice and friendship.

For all those who have lost a loved one as I have... grieve well! Thank you for purchasing this book, and please share it with others.

Glenora

Voyage To The Other Side Of Grief

Table of Contents

Voyage To The Other Side Of Grief

Foreword

"It is possible to learn to live with the hole in your heart."
(Glenora Doherty)

Not very often does any counselor get to hear how a client is doing many years after their meetings. So I am delighted that Glenora asked me to write this brief Foreword to her remarkable account of her "voyage to the other side of grief". I first met Glenora in July of 2007, two years after the death of her husband and at the height of her anxiety facing the challenge of losing yet another member of the family - her wonderful 50-foot sailboat Wanderlust V.

I remember her hard work, her wrestling with challenges, her diligence in completing homework tasks; but mostly I remember her hope… a persistent, searching hope that a brighter day did indeed lie ahead. In this book, Glenora recounts those days as a time of clarification, practical changes and surprising self-discovery. Through her work and her prayer, she has found that by re-engaging with her Christian faith she has sensed God drawing her back to Himself through her painful loss and subsequent 'wilderness'.

"Voyage To The Other Side of Grief" is the inspirational story of a restless soul 'coming home'. In this her first book, Glenora shares her journey of grief through poignant memories and delightful adventures, broken dreams and new beginnings, pitfalls and surprising blessings. Today, she has found acceptance, contentment, hope and new dreams. But it has been a hard and challenging crossing to reach here starting from the very moment she lost Peter, her husband, over six years ago. Glenora shares both the ups and the downs in this book.

You will love such a warm and honest account of her voyage. It is rich in detail and insights from her own experience. You will cry. You will laugh. You will learn about "stages of grief", helpful "steps to survival", yet also how every grief journey is unique. You may well question, along with Glenora, the whole timing of it all. Through her book, Glenora will very likely help you move a little further in your own grief journey…as I realize I have done.

It has been my honour to have had a small part in Glenora's journey. As the English poet, Wordsworth wrote:

> Our birth is but a sleeping and forgetting,
> The soul that rises with us, our life's star,
> Hath had elsewhere its setting,
> And cometh from afar:
> Not in entire forgetfulness,
> And not in utter nakedness,
> But trailing clouds of glory do we come
> From God, who is our home.

What a wonderful homecoming, Peter would be proud. May this book also touch your heart in the ways that it truly matters.

Irene Flett
Registered Clinical Counsellor, Coastal Counselling
Services, Surrey, British Columbia
October, 2011

1

Shattered Dreams

"My beloved Peter – my husband, my lover, my best friend – is gone."
(Journal, May 24, 2005.)

Afternoon, Day 1

Sitting in a private room off the hospital emergency ward with my daughter Tara, I couldn't believe what the tall young doctor was awkwardly and nervously trying to tell us. No! This can't be true! It's not possible! It was so wrong and such a shock that my mind refused to take it in. Only a few hours earlier, over grilled cheese sandwiches for lunch, my husband Peter and I had been chatting about what route we planned to take when we sailed south from Mexico, where our sailing ketch, *Wanderlust V,* was moored awaiting our return from Canada. Peter was on the road to recovery after successful heart surgery just six days earlier. In fact, his cardiologist had assured us he would be able to continue sailing for years. We were in the middle of realizing our life's dream to sail *Wanderlust V,* a boat we'd built ourselves, around the world...

Now, suddenly, Peter was seriously ill. My daughter Tara and I followed the ambulance to Surrey Memorial Hospital and a kind social worker showed us to a small room off the emergency ward, and explained we'd be able to see Peter as soon as they got him settled and did some tests. Then, shortly afterwards, a tall young doctor came in and told me that my husband was a very sick man and that they were applying CPR. He didn't explain further; but I knew this meant that his heart had stopped. Tara and I sobbed and prayed. Now, the doctor was with us again, telling us my beloved husband was gone. I never even got to say goodbye.

I felt numb. Filled with disbelief. The doctor said the medical staff had applied CPR for 15 minutes but had been unable to revive Peter.

"What caused this? How did this happen?" I asked.

The doctor said, "I really don't know. Only an autopsy will reveal the real reason, but we suspect a blood clot entered his lungs."

For the moment, this explanation would have to do. My mind couldn't handle anything more. All I could think about was Peter. He was gone. He was only 61 - so full of life, so passionate about everything he did. How could he be gone? He had so much to do! I needed him. How was I going to live without him? Surely this was just a terrifying nightmare and I'd wake up to find him lying beside me.

For months prior to his scheduled single bypass heart surgery in Canada, I'd been having bad dreams fearing he would die on the operating table. After all, that's always a risk, even if a small one. Peter confessed to me that he'd been having the same nightmares. Even as they were wheeling him in to the operating room and a nurse had asked him how he felt, he'd said, "I'm terrified."

But four hours later he'd come out of surgery smiling, wanting a big kiss and cracking jokes about the staff not having an oxygen mask big enough for a fathead like him. Never in my wildest dreams could I imagine that six days after a totally successful surgery he might suddenly die! He'd not only made it through the surgery with flying colours, but he'd looked so strong, healthy, and tanned from the Mexican sunshine that the nurses said he should be a poster boy for heart surgery. Both of us had been so relieved that he was well, and we would be able to get on with our sailing dream once more. But now…it didn't seem real that he was gone…gone forever! What would I do? What about our dream? What about our boat? Peter's sudden death swept away all certainties and I was overwhelmed.

Tara had called her husband Brian en route to the hospital. He'd come immediately and now he was holding Tara and I, both sobbing uncontrollably. Thinking of my grandchildren, I asked him, "Oh Brian, how are we going to tell T'ea and Matthew?"

"Don't you worry about that. I'll take care of it," he promised me. I'd already called Debbie Judas, Tara's good friend and Associate Pastor at her church, before the ambulance arrived. Debbie had previous experience working in cardiac care and she came immediately to the hospital with another church friend to pray with us. It was a very great comfort that within minutes of Peter's death we were already surrounded by family and friends.

Soon afterwards Tara and I were taken into a curtained-off bed in the ward to see Peter's body. I was grateful when we were told we could stay as long as we wanted. Peter still looked the same grey colour he had when he'd been rushed to hospital in the ambulance. He still had intravenous tubes in one arm and a breathing pipe in his mouth. But his life was gone. His body was already cold. Shuddering, I found his hand and I held it—his big strong hands that were equally competent swinging a hammer or playing the piano, hands that every day had reached out to pull me into one of his big, famous bear hugs or gently caress me. I kissed his forehead. I stroked his beard. And through my tears I gazed at the handsome face I knew as well as the back of my own hands. Tara and I both sat beside him, trying to talk to him, but mostly crying. There is never a good way to say goodbye, but sitting with his body perhaps helped me to recognize that this wonderful man, my beloved husband, father and grandfather to the children he adored, was really gone from us forever.

A nurse took off his rings and took out his clothing from under the gurney. We emptied the pockets of his clothing of all the items he always carried with him: his wallet and watch, loose change, keys, and Swiss army knife. I put them into my pockets. Tara put his engineering ring on her largest finger and handed me his wedding ring. "We can share," she said. I put his wedding ring on my thumb.

As I gazed at that wide gold band, I remembered when he'd first put it on his finger at the jewellery store just eight days earlier, on our 41st anniversary. He'd lost his original wedding ring in the swimming pool in Mazatlan, Mexico, when it slipped off his finger because he'd lost so much weight. When we returned to Vancouver, we went shopping on our anniversary to buy him a new one. As he'd slipped the new ring on his finger he'd said to me, "Now I

3

don't feel naked anymore." When he came home and showed it proudly to Tara, he'd joked, "I'm an honest man again." That evening we went out for a special dinner with our family to celebrate our 41 years of marriage together.

Evening, Day 1

We went home from the hospital to Tara and Brian's house, where Peter and I had been staying since arriving from Mexico just a few short weeks ago, in early May. My grandchildren, T'ea and Matthew, were with Pastor Ian, who had picked them up from school after Brian called him.

When we got home, I sat down calmly and quietly in the living room. But when I glanced across the room and saw Peter's beautiful baby grand piano, I suddenly realized I'd never hear him play it again - and I burst into sobs again. Brian was there immediately holding me. The piano had been in our family for 30 years; bequeathed to Peter by an adopted aunt when Tara was just a baby. It had made dozens of moves with us over the years when Peter was serving in the military. After his retirement in 1984 we settled into a new life in Vancouver, British Columbia. In 1994 after Tara was married and our son Ryan was already off on his own, we became empty nesters. So three weeks after Tara's wedding, Peter and I moved aboard *Wanderlust V*, our Reliance 44 ketch. Ever since then, Tara and Brian had "stored" the baby grand for us in their living room. Whenever we came to visit, Peter loved to play it.

Peter had played the piano every day of his life since he started lessons at age five. We even built in a marine piano on the boat, knowing we planned to live aboard and he knew he couldn't live without a piano. I loved to listen to him play. In fact, we made a deal - I would happily do the dishes every night if he would play the piano while I worked in the galley. And he'd always end with my favourite number. Whenever we invited cruising friends over for coffee or a drink, Peter would be more than happy to play for them. We hosted some wonderful music parties when other cruisers brought their guitars, banjos, harmonicas, and voices. Once, we even had a harp on board. Seeing the piano in Tara's living room and knowing that I would never again hear him play for me was overwhelming and heartbreaking. How was I going to live without him? Or his music?

My husband's death hit our grandchildren hard too. When eight-year-old Matthew came in the door, he said to his Mom, "I know! Poppa went to the hospital again, and now he's dead." He said it so clearly and matter of factly, you'd think he was giving a weather report.

That was probably his coping mechanism; loudly assuring everyone he didn't need to be told, because he didn't *want* to hear it again. It wasn't until about a week later that Matthew finally succumbed. We were all at a friend's house for dinner and when we noticed Matthew was missing, Tara went looking for him. He had crawled into a very small dark place under the stairs down in the basement and was crying his little heart out for the beloved Poppa he worshipped and adored.

Ten-year-old T'ea kept wandering about, looking lost, but whenever she saw me she'd come and give me a hug. Tara later discovered that she was crying by herself in the bathroom, because she was afraid if she cried in front of us, she'd make us more sad. She has always been such a sensitive, thoughtful little girl, like her Mom.

We tried to explain to T'ea and Matthew that tears were good, that they honoured and praised their Poppa's life, and that they helped us wash out our sorrow and get rid of it, just like tears wash away a speck of dust that irritates the eye.

The loss of a loved one throws every aspect of our lives out of balance. The closer we were to the person who died the more havoc the loss creates. Love does not die quickly. Hence to grieve is also to celebrate the depth of the union. Tears are the jewels of remembrance, sad but glistening with the beauty of the past. So grief in its bitterness marks the end... but it also is praise to the one who is gone.

(Anon.)

The phone kept ringing. Brian kept answering, taking messages and calling people. What a guy! Every time any of us talked on the phone, the call waiting beep alerted us more calls were coming in, but we didn't break off our conversations. Brian checked messages when he could. It was grand central station, with phones ringing, people coming and going, sobbing and hugging. Several of Tara's friends managed to pull together a spaghetti dinner for everyone at the house. I was surprised I could eat that first night without Peter, but I did.

Many of the phone calls coming in were from friends and members of Bluewater Cruising Association (BCA). Shortly after Peter's retirement from the military in 1984, we discovered BCA, a Canadian non-profit society formed in 1978 to promote offshore sailing. BCA has about 900 members, with chapters in Vancouver, Victoria and Calgary. We became active members. Peter was a Past Commodore and I had edited BCA's monthly magazine, *Currents*, for seven years, so we came in contact with many of the members, not only at meetings, but also on the water. We were both well known in the organization. The cruising friends we made became a family to us, just like our military friends had been.

Our first boat was a canoe we took on camping trips before the children were born and the second a runabout we used for water skiing. When we discovered sailing, we bought a Sunfish sailboard, and then in 1976 when we moved to California, we bought our fourth boat, *Wanderlust IV*, an Ericson 32 sloop. On that boat, our whole family fell in love with the cruising lifestyle, so in 1980 we sold the Ericson and bought a Reliance 44 bare hull and spent eight years building it to seaworthy condition. *Wanderlust V* took us, our two teenagers and our pet dog on our first wonderful offshore voyage in 1989-90. When the two of us retired and left Canada on our second offshore trip in 2002, we became part of an even larger cruising community due to the fact that Peter became the chief net controller for the Bluewater Single Sideband (SSB) Net.

Two Happy Clams, Monterey CA Aquarium, 2002

The day Peter passed away, I made one phone call to the Secretary for BCA who was a good friend; she and the executive arranged to get the word out quickly in a broadcast email message to the 900+ members of BCA. The members, in turn, forwarded the information to other cruisers located all over the world, by email or by making announcements on their respective SSB and Ham radio nets. The Editor even stopped the presses on the June issue of *Currents* to insert a "Passages" column about Peter. This is the email I personally sent out to over 200 of our friends:

My Broadcast Email to Friends and Family

Dear Friends,

I am devastated to share that my beloved husband, Peter Doherty, passed away suddenly May 24th, 2005. He had had bypass surgery on the 18th of May, and made a spectacular recovery. This last week he has been filled with energy and joy he has not had in over a year... the passionate energetic man we had missed was back in fine form! He even insisted on walking to church this last Sunday saying, "We've got a lot to celebrate!" and the next day he was out mowing the lawn.

On Tuesday afternoon, he was sitting at his computer responding to the many well wishing emails he'd received since coming home from the hospital, when he suddenly went into distress. Despite being rushed to hospital and the immediate and tireless efforts of paramedics and doctors, he passed away less than an hour later. The actual cause of his sudden and unexpected death is yet to be confirmed by autopsy, but the attending doctor believes a blood clot went into his lungs. Whatever the reason, I will be forever grateful that he died a happy man. His death was quick and in his unconscious state he was likely unaware of any pain. It was just much too soon. He had so much left to do...

I have no idea how I will live without him. We'd been high school sweethearts; he was my life's soul mate, lover, and best friend. Two days before his surgery, we celebrated our 41st anniversary. We were a team in everything we did, and we did absolutely everything together. I now face the biggest challenge of my life... figuring out who I am, what I want to do with the rest of my life, and where... without him.

Fortunately, I am surrounded by my wonderful children and grandchildren and many friends. Four years ago, Peter and I shared the purchase of our daughter's house in Surrey, BC. There is a lovely two-bedroom in-law suite on the bottom floor, which has been rented out while we've been cruising, but next month it will become my home base for at least the next year, until I can decide where else I'd rather be. I don't yet know when or by what route, but with the help of my son and many good Bluewater friends, I will likely be bringing *Wanderlust V* back to Vancouver within the next year. At that time, Peter will go for one last sail and his ashes will be sprinkled at sea.

Please keep in touch. To our Mexico cruising friends, I miss you all so much, and wish I was there with you. I also miss *Wanderlust V*, our home for the last 11 years. A local man has been hired to maintain her in our absence, but if any of you are in Mazatlan or passing through, I would very much appreciate reports from you that she's OK. Good cruising!
Glenora

My message came as such a terrific shock to all our friends because just the morning before Peter had been busy emailing them all with the good news of his successful bypass heart surgery. Here are Peter's last written words:

Dear Friends,
Thank you so much for your kind words and wishes. The two of us are facing each other; sitting at our respective computers trying to clear our correspondence from both e-mail systems. Some of it dates back over two months.

The big news is that I (Peter) am home already! They booted me out of the hospital on Saturday morning, less than 72 hours after being wheeled into the OR. Thanks to an incredible surgical team and their sophisticated procedure, I have only a tidy four-inch row of staples on my upper left chest to show for the experience *and* I'm far more chipper than I ever expected to be at this juncture. (He was mowing the lawn yesterday! G.) We're very relieved and feel like a major corner has been turned.

Our plans for this summer include attending the Bluewater Rendezvous at Montague Harbour at the end of July, and attending the June and September Bluewater Club Nights. Also in September, we're off to a reunion of Air Force Aerospace Engineering officers and to my 40th anniversary homecoming at University of Alberta. Until then, we'll be enjoying the lovely

BC coastal summer weather, visiting friends and family here and on the Island.

Barring the unexpected, we'll fly back to Mazatlan on October 6th and get as far north into the Sea of Cortez as we can before the northers set in. Only another medical delay is likely to change that (God forbid!). La Paz for Christmas and the South Pacific next spring. All plans are, of course, indelibly etched in Jell-O…. Thanks.

Peter & Glenora, at home with the family in Surrey, BC Tuesday, May 24, 2005

Understanding the Stages of Grief

The shock and denial I was going through immediately after Peter's death were part of what we can call the first stage in the grief process. There are several stages of grief that have become standards in helping people who are grieving to understand what's happening to them. They don't have to be understood rigidly but in my own long voyage to the other side of grief I have found the insights helpful and reassuring that I'm not alone in the often overwhelming waves of emotions.

The Seven Stages of Grief
1. Shock and Denial
2. Pain and Guilt
3. Anger and Bargaining (blaming someone)
4. Depression, Reflection, Loneliness
5. The Upward Turn
6. Reconstruction and Working Through
7. Acceptance and Hope

Elizabeth Kubler-Ross first identified five stages (denial, anger, bargaining, depression, acceptance) in her 1969 book, *On Death and Dying*. However, her book was intended for cancer patients who were dying, not for the grieving loved ones left behind.

Many other descriptions of the processes and stages of grief have emerged since Kubler-Ross's pioneering work, including the seven-stage model described on www.recover-from-grief.com. This is a very helpful website maintained by Jenny Wright, a registered nurse and certified grief counsellor with 20 years of experience. She explained to me that the "stages of grief" are strictly theory, not scientific fact. Her model is based upon her clinical experience and advanced studies of the medical, psychological, and sociological aspects of death and the ways in which people deal with death. I personally prefer this seven-stage model to describe my own voyage because it includes two extra, very positive steps, the "Upward Turn" and "Reconstruction and Working Through" before the final stage, "Acceptance and Hope".

On that very first day after Peter died I realized that every time I was overcome with tears, I was experiencing a "wave of grief". I'd heard this phrase used before and never quite understood it. Now I did. I could be sitting discussing the weather, or even smiling, when I'd see something or a memory would flash through my mind that reminded me of Peter and grief would wash and tumble over me like a huge ocean wave. I'd be overwhelmed. I'd cringe and shudder and start to drown in uncontrollable sobs. The wave would block out everything around me except the shock, disbelief and denial of death itself.

Jenny Wright defines Stage 1 as follows:

> **Stage 1 of Grief - Shock & Denial:** Probably, you will react to learning of the loss with numbed disbelief. You may deny the reality of the loss, at some level, in order to avoid the pain. Shock provides emotional protection from being overwhelmed. This may last for weeks.

Generally, intense grief reactions are displayed in the first six to eight weeks following the death. However, sometimes a person may skip a stage altogether. For example, I don't think I ever felt anger (Stage 3) - or at least very little anger - about Peter's death. Yes, I was confused and in despair, but I couldn't blame anyone. I just had questions. Why did Peter have to leave me now? What caused his death? What was I going to do?...A little voice inside me, which I tried to ignore initially - but now believe was God's voice - told me that He had some other wonderful plans for me. I just had no idea what they were. My future without Peter scared me - a lot!

Steps to Survival – Stage 1

- ❖ Recognize the loss. For a while you are numb. It has happened; try not to avoid it. You're hurting. Admit it.
- ❖ To feel pain after loss is normal, proof that you are alive. This is *good*. You are not alone.
- ❖ Loss is a part of life – *Everyone* experiences it sooner or later.
- ❖ Know that you are a beautiful, worthwhile person. You are much more than the emotional wound you are presently feeling.
- ❖ Do your mourning now. Allow yourself to be with your pain. It will pass sooner. Postponed grief can return to haunt you later and hurt you further.
- ❖ Be gentle with yourself: You have suffered a deep disabling emotional wound. Treat yourself with compassion and gentle care.
- ❖ Crying is cleansing and a wonderful release.
- ❖ Heal at your own pace. Never compare yourself to any other grieving person. Each of us has our own time clock.

2
Reality

Blessed are those who mourn, for they will be comforted.
(Matthew 5:4)

Introduction

After the death of a family member, there are a number of immediate and unavoidable realities of life (and death) that must be dealt with. The grieving process continues, even with all the necessary daily activities and errands that must be attended to. You may not feel like it - I know I sometimes found it hard to cope with a daily to-do list - but having to get up every morning, prepare meals, make phone calls, write emails, pay bills and go to appointments, all contributed to my gradual recovery.

The first thing that needs to be done is to plan and prepare for a funeral or memorial service. We decided it would be a Celebration of Life service, because Peter had indeed lived an incredible life, worthy of celebration. However, this was a huge undertaking for our family. Most importantly, our son Ryan was living and working in Peru as a volunteer English teacher so we couldn't schedule a service until we knew when he could arrive. Ryan had to make a number of arrangements, the most difficult of which was the need to renew his passport.

In addition, until we knew the date of the service, we couldn't even publish an obituary. Because we'd lived in so many places, the obituary would have to be placed in several newspapers: Vancouver, Victoria, Calgary and Ottawa at a minimum. The other major task was to find a venue large enough to host Peter's Celebration of Life service. While we waited to hear from Ryan, we did what we could to prepare for the service, such as drafting an obituary and scanning photographs from albums for a slide show presentation illustrating Peter's life.

During this time, my immediate family and friends stayed close to me and made sure I never slept alone. That first night after Peter's death, my sweet 10-year-old granddaughter T'ea said, "You can sleep with me tonight, Grandma." My daughter Tara and I stayed up crying, talking and hugging each other until nearly 5 am but it was wonderful finally to crawl in bed beside T'ea's small warm body and cuddle, rather than try to sleep alone in the big bed Peter and I had shared the previous night. Without Peter, or my darling granddaughter to comfort me, that bed would just have been too empty for me to sleep alone. That same night, my grandson Matthew brought his Mommy Bloo, his favourite bedtime teddy bear, so she wouldn't be sad. For the next two nights, girlfriends from out of town arrived and each took turns making sure that I was not alone at night.

My Son Arrives from Peru

> Ryan came through the arrivals door at Vancouver International Airport pushing his luggage in a cart and there in the cart was a baby – *Daryan*, my new grandson! What a surprise! I was so excited to meet and hold Daryan for the first time, I could scarcely believe he was here with Ryan. And he is so beautiful— big brown eyes, soft thick brown hair, long eyelashes, and big smiles. I don't think I stopped smiling for nearly two hours! (Journal, May 29, 2005**.**)

The whole story I'd been told about Ryan being delayed because his passport needed to be renewed was a cover-up invented by my son and daughter in order to give me a lovely surprise. When I heard Ryan was coming, I was so happy and relieved and looking forward to having his arms around me, that I never even questioned why it took only five days. I never imagined the surprise they were planning for me. The real delay was getting a temporary passport for one-year-old Daryan for his first trip outside Peru, where he'd been born.

That night Ryan slept with me, with Daryan between the two of us. What a joy! I wrote in my journal that I was happy about something, only five days after Peter's death. It was the first small glimmer of hope that I would survive, and that, after a long voyage of grief, I would be okay. I've always felt that family really is everything. To be surrounded and loved by my children and grandchildren when otherwise I felt so terribly alone was a tremendous support and consolation. I think they felt the same. In the salon of *Wanderlust V*, Peter and I had a little blue pillow Tara had given me as a gift. It had a silver heart in the middle engraved with the words, "Family are the friends we keep forever."

It wasn't until much later the significance of the situation really hit home. Daryan was the one who would carry on Peter's name for future generations. Peter and I had both felt incredibly honoured that our son's only son was named after him (Daryan Peter Doherty-Salas), and that our daughter's only daughter was named after me (T'ea Glenora Dong). Unfortunately, Peter never even got to meet Daryan. We'd seen photographs of him, but we hadn't been able to fly to Peru to meet him personally as we had for his big sister, Angie, when she had been born two years earlier.

Angie stayed home in Peru with her other grandmother, but daughter-in-law Jackie arrived on her own – and just in time - one day before Peter's service, to join Ryan and Daryan. She came as soon as she could get a visitor's visa. Like Daryan, it was the first time she'd ever been outside Peru, and her very first trip on an airplane. Fortunately, she spoke excellent English, so she was comfortable asking for help and directions on her international flight alone. She had taught English to children in Peru, which is how she and Ryan met.

Planning Meeting for the Celebration of Life Service

Once Ryan arrived from Peru and a venue had been found for Peter's Celebration of Life Service, we could set the date and get the obituary into newspapers in Victoria, Vancouver, Calgary and Ottawa, as well as on our own website. Tara's pastor, Ian Lopez, was asked to officiate the service, and his compassion and sense of humour were wonderful. I knew Peter would approve. When we had visited New Beginnings Community Church with Tara, we had heard Ian speak numerous times and Peter had mentioned that he really liked Ian and respected him.

Ian put everyone at ease at a brief planning meeting in Tara and Brian's living room, but kept us focused on organizing the service. The Past Commodore of Bluewater Cruising Association would speak about Peter's 30+ years as a sailor; a good friend and former military colleague would speak about Peter's 25-year military career; and Ryan would speak about what his Dad had meant to him. There was a lot I wanted to say too, but I knew I'd be incoherent with tears during the service, so Tara said she'd speak for me, if I would write the words for her to read. At the end of the meeting , my granddaughter T'ea offered to read a scripture that she had picked out herself.

Peter's Piano Music

When we thought about what music to have for the service, Peter's own beautiful piano music was the first that came to mind. It seemed a perfect gift we could offer everyone. Years ago, he'd recorded a cassette tape and I suspected that his Mom in Calgary, Alberta, might still have the original. His sister Jennifer found it and brought it with her when she arrived in Vancouver a week before the service. A friend of Tara's who professionally produces videos cleaned up the tape and arranged it in tracks on a CD. Tara, a talented graphic artist, designed the cover, playlist and insert for the CD. I wrote the story behind the CD:

> Originally recorded by Peter on his own baby grand piano in our home in 1985, 'Variations on a Theme' was created as a birthday gift for his father, and later served as a demo tape for his professional music career.
>
> While many of the pieces on this CD have been written, performed and popularized by well-known artists, all of the arrangements are Peter's very own. Also included are two of his original compositions: "Peter's Thoughts of Home" and

"Whimsy in E♭". He never wrote any of his arrangements down; they were just indelibly committed to his memory. Fortunately, this one recording has captured them, so they will live on.

Peter started playing piano at age five. He completed his classical training through the Royal Toronto Conservatory of Music before going on, at age 16, to study popular music and improvisation under Jac Friedenberg in Calgary, Alberta. This broad teaching and experience, combined with Peter's love for his music, left a unique imprint on every piece he played.

In the early 1970s, Peter heard a piano selection on the car radio that changed his life. It was so familiar he felt it could have been his own music. His excitement about that music led him to call the radio station in search of the song and composer's name. The song he heard was "Storm Warning" by Frank Mills. In the years that followed, Peter searched out and learned all of Frank's music. Not surprisingly, once he had learned each piece from sheet music, his creativity and perfectionism took over, and he adapted it to his own style and committed it to memory.

Although this CD was created in the days that followed Peter's sudden and unexpected death on May 24, 2005, the vision for it was actually his. A fellow sailor in Mexico, who was a concert pianist, gave him a CD of her music, and Peter realized he could do the same thing – create a CD of his music as a small and personal gift to express his thanks to those who were helping him along life's journey.

To all my dear family and friends, I can think of nothing more fitting for me to leave you with than the sound of Peter's music. Please accept this CD gift as my heartfelt thanks to you for your overwhelming love and support. Enjoy!
Glenora Doherty

The CDs of Peter's music were going to be handed out to each couple or family attending the service as they arrived and Peter's piano music would be played over the sound system as people entered the sanctuary before the service, as well as during the digital slide presentation during the service. Yes, with the help of many people, Peter would play for his own funeral. He'd have loved that!

It was so like him. He played at his daughter's wedding too. The memory of that makes me smile...Thank you, my love.

> One of the funniest things that happened today at Tara's wedding was that Peter was so busy watching the clock and organizing everyone else getting dressed at a friend's home and into vehicles to get to the church on time, that he forgot to put on his own bow tie. There he was... dressed in his tux, pleated white dress shirt with gold cuff links and cummerbund, but no tie! He walked his daughter up the aisle, gave her away, then replaced his friend at the organ and played the music for the rest of the service. It wasn't until we started taking group photographs after the service that someone noticed he didn't have his tie on. He was absolutely mortified. (Journal, April 23, 1994.)

Arranging a Venue and Program

Other funeral arrangements involved choosing a venue, or in our case more than one venue, and designing a program for the service. It's important to choose a venue – church, community centre, yacht club, funeral home, etc. - that the deceased would have approved. It's also necessary to choose a central location that is easy to locate and a place that provides adequate seating, parking, and the ability to cater a reception. Finding a venue for Peter's service had not been easy, as we knew we'd need a large place to accommodate everybody. We finally found a sister church to New Beginnings Community Church that could accommodate 350, had lots of parking, and could cater a reception with a light lunch and beverages.

We also visited the funeral home where his body would be cremated. I took Peter's will with me that showed I was his trustee and therefore could sign the papers authorizing his cremation. We were shown an appropriate room where we could have a small private family viewing a few days prior to the Celebration of Life Service.

Accommodation and transportation arrangements had to be made for out-of-town guests and family arriving from Peru, California, Washington, Oregon, Saskatchewan, Alberta, and of course from various centers in British Columbia. Brian was kept busy ferrying guests from the hotel to the house for meals and visits and back again to the hotel to sleep.

Although the church was appropriate for Peter and could accommodate everyone, no wine or alcoholic beverages were permitted to toast the deceased. I knew Peter would be rolling over in his grave at the thought of a celebration without a drink. The first thing he always said to any guests when they entered our home or boarded our boat was, "What would you like to drink?" We had a fully stocked bar on board, built right into the salon table. (And of course, we also had a thermos of coffee, soft drinks and fruit juices available.) Peter told me once that an Irish Wake was the only proper way to celebrate anyone's passing. So we arranged for a second event to be held the same day, after Peter's official Celebration of Life service at the church. It would be held at the Spruce Harbour Marina lounge in False Creek, Vancouver, British Columbia, courtesy of friends and former neighbours who lived aboard there.

When Blake Williams, another Past Commodore of BCA, called to offer his condolences and asked what he could do to help, I asked him to MC the reception that we were planning to follow the church service. When I told him about the wake we were planning, he mentioned he could probably round up a fiddle and accordion players to perform some Irish jigs and sea shanties.

For the service, Tara created a beautiful program using a design from one of the condolence cards I received – a compass drawn in the sand on a beach and an excellent photograph of Peter that a friend had taken just two weeks earlier. There were so many other arrangements to be made, that I recall we were folding the hot-off-the-press programs as we drove to the church the day of Peter's service.

Being busy helped all of us. It gave me something to do that made me feel I was contributing to the service that would honour Peter and to allow all his family and friends to pay their respects. It also made me realize what a wonderful support network was out there, especially my immediate family. I was never alone. My family was just "there" for me.

During the sometimes hectic days after Peter's death, one of the great comforts was the often unspoken support friends and even strangers gave to our family. For example, friends from Tara's church brought us meals every day. Sometimes we had so many casseroles or prepared meals that we had to freeze them and keep them for another day. Another church family gave us the use of their seven-passenger van for several days to transport family and friends to and from the airport and to the Celebration of Life Service. When other church members discovered that Ryan had arrived with his one-year-old son, a playpen and a highchair arrived at the front door. The outpouring of love, caring and support was overwhelming.

Memories in Photographs

Preparing the slide show for the service was an enormous task because most of the photographs were not digital, just prints pulled from family albums. However, it was worth the effort. Tara set up a scanner on the dining room table, and everyone in the house took turns scanning pictures whenever they had a moment. Then Tara put them together into a beautiful slide presentation, showing pictures of Peter throughout his life, from the time he was a wee baby. She added title slides and short captions so no narration would be required, just Peter's piano music playing in the background.

The Viewing - June 1, 2005

Prior to the service and before Peter's body was cremated, we decided we should have a small private family viewing at the funeral home, as there were immediate family members, especially Ryan, who hadn't seen him just before he died.

The funeral director asked us to deliver appropriate clothes for

Wanderlust V in Banderos Bay Sail Past 2003

Peter's body for the viewing. Looking through his clothing not only renewed our grief, it also caused a small dilemma. During his military career, he always said he wanted to be buried in his officer's mess kit, so we pulled it out of storage. Later, when he became a sailor, he'd also said he wanted to be cremated and to have his ashes scattered on the ocean. After debating for a while, we chose the Hawaiian wedding shirt he'd bought in Honolulu, Hawaii, on our first offshore trip. It was a white cotton casual shirt but had lace inserts on the three-quarter length sleeves and the collar. He often wore it, along with white pants, for dress-up occasions when we were cruising.

He had worn the exact same outfit to the Awards Dinner for the Banderas Bay Regatta in Nuevo Vallarta, Mexico, in 2003, when *Wanderlust V* won 1st place in the non-spinnaker cruising category (*1er lugar Clase G*) and received an honourable mention for "looking good!" in the sail past. I had worn my Tilley silk burgundy jacket and long skirt to the Awards Dinner. So it was fitting that I chose the same burgundy jacket and skirt for his Celebration of Life Service. However, I have to admit that I've never had the courage to wear it since. It no longer reminds me of an awards ceremony celebration; it reminds me of his funeral.

Going to the funeral home to see his body felt strange, but it was good for Tara and me to see him again one more time. He looked so peaceful, even the usual furrow of his brow was gone and the beginning of a smile on his lips. He looked more like himself than the last glimpse I had of him in the hospital. Ryan, Tara and I went in first, then Brian brought in the kids and Peter's sister, Jennifer, and finally some long-time dear friends who came from Washington but couldn't stay for the service. The kids were so good. Each of them had drawn cute pictures with loving words to put beside him in his cremation box. T'ea's said "Great Poppa". They went right up to see him with their Mom and Dad, said goodbye to him, and then sat with their Mom and cried. The cremation box was much like a wooden coffin, with one-half of the lid open so we could see him lying there peacefully with his arms across his chest. His actual ashes, once cremated, were put in another box that was made of biodegradable materials so once the ashes had been scattered on the ocean, the entire box could be thrown in the water as well. Peter would have approved of that too!

We all shed tears of course, but afterwards, Tara and I had to relate the story about the first time little Matthew saw his Poppa wearing this white shirt and Peter explained to him that this was his Hawaiian wedding shirt. Matthew asked, "Oh... so who you gonna marry?" Peter had roared with laughter and we laughed too, recalling that moment between a little boy and his grandfather. Talking about a happy memory felt good.

The Celebration of Life Service - June 6, 2005

As people arrived at the Celebration of Life Service, they signed a guest book at the entrance and were handed the CD of Peter's music. As planned, his music was playing as they entered the sanctuary, as well as during the slide presentation and at the end of the service as they left.

The service was beautiful, not only because of our collective planning and preparations, but because of the people who were there. It took great courage to walk down the aisle, leading my family in, my son at my side, and seeing so many familiar faces that represented the many phases of my husband's life. There were Boy

Scout Leaders there in uniform, even though it had been over 15 years since Peter had volunteered for that organization; there were cruising sailors we had met in Mexico who had driven up from Washington and Oregon; and a whole bus load of BCA members had come over on the ferry from Vancouver Island. I noticed my cousins who had flown in from Saskatchewan and former colleagues I had worked with in Victoria, British Columbia, before I retired.

Silently praying for courage and strength, I managed to keep my chin up, made eye contact and nodded my head at many of these people, giving them a small nervous smile of thanks, and reached my seat at the front of the church with dry eyes. However, the sadness and sympathy on their faces was very evident, and it made me realize the impact my husband had had on others, that they would make such a huge effort to come. It pleased me to know how many people there were that remembered Peter and admired him. I was not alone in my sorrow.

Ian gave opening words and a prayer, then lead us all in singing one of Peter's favourite hymns, *How Great Thou Art*, followed by T'ea's scripture. I was incredibly touched when she explained that she had chosen this particular scripture because in the last year of his life, her Poppa had always been tired and weak (due to a prescribed medication that slowed down his heart).

But those who wait on the Lord will find new strength. They will fly high on wings like eagles. They will run and not grow weary. They will walk and not grow faint.
(Isaiah 40:31)

Ryan's Eulogy

My father and I had a complicated and loving relationship...He poured vast amounts of love, information and energy into me even though I often thought I disappointed him. I used to think he was such an impatient man, but truth be told, anyone who could put up with me had more patience than I can measure. I was a child...then a teenager...and finally a man - of opinions

23

and arguments - who seldom took advice or did what I was told to do. In spite of all this, he never quit on me…that is how I measure his life.

People have asked me what I will miss most about my father. I've enjoyed working with tools my whole life. As a child, I saw my father, as a boy does, as the definitive source of all knowledge. So when my father's list of weekend chores included tightening a hinge or replacing a part on the car, or my favourite job - working on *Wanderlust V* - I would always volunteer to be Dad's helper. I was an eager boy wanting to use a screwdriver or a wrench and as time went on – power tools! And my father never disappointed me. He would let me take the screwdriver in my inexperienced hand and make the initial unsteady passes, watching, as with each turn, my hand grew steadier and stronger. And then, when the screw or bolt was almost in – just at the point when I was really building up a good rhythm and beginning to bear down with all my 10-year-old strength, my father would say, **"Don't force it!"**

Looking back, I can't remember all the projects, but I do remember those words, repeated time and time again. And to this very day, when I'm laying on my back under a car or fixing something I hear those words – Don't force it! – as I bear down on the wrench…

The loss of my father has been painful, yet also strangely reaffirming, because it has made me ever more aware of the rewards of our wonderful partnership. Perhaps the most consoling words came from a Peruvian friend who has known me for less than three years. He said, "Think of the legacy he left you -- a curiosity about life, a hunger for knowledge and to see the world, a passion for helping others, an example of a life whose riches owe little to money, a sense that anything is possible if you work hard, a model of what a father and friend should be. *Todos fueron muy buenos regalos."* (These are all great

24

gifts.) My father was everything I aspired to be, in my own way. He did that for me and because he did, we will always travel together.

Together today we mourn. We remember the man; we take the measure of his life. We celebrate the memories of his love, and the gift of his life. And throughout my life, his voice will come to me – as it does when I'm tightening the wrench – Don't force it! Thank you, Dad, for these gifts!

This is the tribute that Tara read from me:

Glenora's Tribute to Peter

Peter and I met each other in Grade 10 gym class when we were 15. The sport was dancing, and to choose partners, the girls and boys were lined up facing each other, shortest to tallest. However, somehow the lines got turned around and Peter, the tallest boy in the class (6'2"), wound up dancing with the shortest girl (5'0") - which was me! We became best friends, and then sweethearts. One of our teachers called us 'Mutt and Jeff,' and teased us, 'It'll never last.' Little did he know we would celebrate 41 years of marriage, before Peter was suddenly taken from me.

Peter was many things, but to me his most endearing quality, and the one that initially made me fall in love with him, was the way he was always ready to drop everything to help a friend – or sometimes even a perfect stranger. He was the ultimate Good Samaritan. Every time he visited his mother in Calgary, she had a list of things ready for him that needed fixing, and he was thrilled and quick to help. If another cruiser came up on one of the radio nets with a request for advice, assistance, or the loan of a tool, Peter was the first to offer to help. As a Mechanical Engineer, practical things were his strength. He had more trouble with emotional problems, because often there was no quick fix. If I had a headache, his first question was, 'Have you taken an aspirin?' I tried for years to teach him that just listening, saying he was sorry, and giving me a hug, helped just as much as a pill or a band aid. And he was learning. He was getting there. I just needed a little more time…

Part of being a helpful friend was being a generous friend. Our home, our dinner table and our bar were always open to visitors - from the formal five-course sit down dinners we served in our home when he was a senior military officer, to the potluck dinners we had in shorts and t-shirts aboard *Wanderlust V*. He learned to make really good margaritas while we were in Mexico, and in the last few years, there was nothing he enjoyed more than hosting a margarita party aboard *Wanderlust V*. The first excuse was when he finished installing the freezer. By then, we were already in Mexico at Magdalena Bay. We made bags of ice cubes and invited everyone in the anchorage to come to a margarita party on board.

He was always a romantic and a gentleman. He carried my books to school, insisted on opening doors for me, walking on the street side of the sidewalk when we walked together, and preceding me down stairways holding my hand. He'd often surprise me with flowers or some small gift for no reason at all. The year before we were married, he came knocking at my window late one night following an RCAF mess dinner, with a long-stemmed red rose clenched between his teeth. And sometimes when he had a gift for me, he couldn't wait to give it to me. His last gift to me was a beautiful silver statue of a mariachi singer. I'd admired it every time I went in to a gift shop at El Cid Marina in Mazatlan and he managed to sneak it home in his luggage as an anniversary gift. But the day we got home and I started handing out our gifts to the kids, he just had to bring out his anniversary gift for me – 12 days early. He said, "I thought this guy would get lonely without you visiting him."

I know he loved me deeply. He told me every day by his words and his actions. He loved all his family. In addition, we both loved *Wanderlust V* with a passion. He loved Canada and proudly flew the biggest possible maple leaf flag on our boat. He loved his music. He loved a good strong cup of black coffee, Scotch on the rocks, popcorn, avocados, a rare steak, and black cherry ice cream. Peter loved life.

Most of you know how much we were looking forward to the next phase of our journey on *Wanderlust V* across the South Pacific. With help from my Bluewater friends and family, maybe I'll still do it; maybe I won't. When we launched *Wanderlust V* in 1988, our dream was to live aboard and cruise extensively. We've done that. We've now lived aboard for 13 years and sailed 29,000 miles together. I have memories to last a lifetime. He's left me with some precious gifts: our loving and caring children and beautiful grandchildren; his masterpiece, *Wanderlust V*; and his music. These are his legacies.

Slide Show Presentation

The slide show presentation of photographs came at the end of the Celebration of Life service and brought back so many memories. There was a picture of Peter in his RCAF Officer Cadet's uniform, heading off to the Officer's Training Course in Centralia, Ontario, the first summer after Peter and I graduated from high school. He completed his engineering degree from the University of Alberta, through the Regular Officers' Training Plan, and on graduation became a commissioned officer in the RCAF, serving on bases, wings and detachments in five different Canadian provinces, as well as postings to Germany and California. It was while Peter was serving in Germany that we discovered the joy of travel; our wanderlust was not only born, but became our wholehearted way of life.

Most of the slides in the presentation consisted of sailing pictures. It had been the centre of our lives for over 30 years. Our first sailing experience was in 1973 on a friend's 17-foot Siren day sailor. Soon afterwards, we bought a Sunfish sailboard, and when Peter was transferred to California in 1976, we bought our first real cruising sailboat, *Wanderlust IV*, an Ericson 32 sloop. We spent every weekend and holiday for the next four years cruising the California Channel Islands and coastline with our two

RCAF Officer Cadet Peter Doherty, 1962

toddlers and pet dog. As a family, we fell in love with the cruising lifestyle, and decided we wanted a larger boat that we could live aboard as a family and cruise extensively.

Glenora on Wanderlust IV with Ryan & Tara 1978

We sold *Wanderlust IV* in California, and bought an empty 44-foot hull from Reliance Sailcraft in Montreal in 1980. It was delivered to our home in Ottawa in June of that year. *Wanderlust V* was the boat that became Peter's masterpiece and which he referred to as his "unfinished symphony". We spent eight years fitting her out from a bare hull until she was a comfortable and very seaworthy yacht that took us safely up and down the coast of British Columbia and offshore with our two teenagers and pet dog, to Mexico, Hawaii, Alaska and back to Vancouver in 1989-90. We spent Christmas 1989 in Channel Islands Harbour, in Oxnard, California.

Family Christmas Aboard Wanderlust V 1989

In that one year, we covered 11,000 nautical miles. Although *Wanderlust V* was fully equipped and prepared to sail across oceans, she was still unfinished because we enjoyed sailing more than building. After living aboard and cruising since her launch in 1988, at the time of Peter's death, we still hadn't completed many of the cosmetic finishing touches in the interior, such as a headliner, a teak and holly sole (floor) or trim strips. But on the outside, her sleek white hull and distinctive tanbark sails were beautiful. Furthermore, she could really sail well and fast!

We all enjoyed that offshore trip so much, we knew we wanted to go again someday, but not on a one-year schedule. We needed to be financially secure so that it would be an open-ended voyage. So we both went back to work to build up our pensions. When the kids left home a few years later, we moved aboard full-time and sailed every weekend and holiday; always dreaming of the day we'd head offshore again.

Peter, BCA SSB Net Control, 2002

When the two of us retired and left Canada to go on our second offshore trip in 2002, we became part of an even larger cruising community due to the fact that Peter became the chief net controller for the Bluewater Single Sideband (SSB) Net. The Net originally started in Victoria, British Columbia, for the benefit of those BCA members heading offshore in 2002, with local members hosting the net. We'd share useful information, such as weather, other navigational tips and our current position. Because we knew who was sailing where, it was easy to meet up frequently with each other along the way. This informal network of cruising sailors became our new social network. When our fleet of about 12 boats from Canada reached San Francisco, Peter volunteered to take over as net control in order to keep the Net going until we all reached Mexico safely. Word spread, and by the time we got to San Diego, with Peter's naturally gregarious and inclusive manner, we had over 75 cruising boats checking in nightly, many of whom were not BCA members nor Canadians.

What fun it was when we got into an anchorage and spotted a boat whose name we recognized as one of those who checked in with us. Of course we would immediately hop into our dinghy, row over and say hello - if they didn't manage to come and visit us first. In which case, they'd usually say something like, "*So you're Wanderlust V!* We've heard you on the net and just wanted to meet the face behind the voice." Many of the cruising friends we met through the net became lifelong friends.

After the slide show at the end of the service, Mom Doherty and I led the procession of family out of the church and greeted everyone in the lobby. All I could manage was to hug each one and thank them for coming. The line was so long, that the MC finally started the reception without me and I had to scurry apologetically past several people who had been waiting in line. There was an open microphone for anyone to get up and say a few words about Peter and there were some wonderfully funny and touching stories told.

We were all exhausted when we got home. I did lie down for a bit before I changed, but didn't sleep. Finally I assembled those who were going to the wake – Mom Doherty, Ryan, four other family members and me - all in the 7-passenger van lent to us by church friends.

An Irish Wake

That evening, as planned, Peter's Wake was held at the Spruce Harbour Marina lounge in Vancouver's False Creek. The deck off the second-floor lounge looked out over the boats on the docks where we had once moored *Wanderlust V*. We lived aboard there from 1994 to 1997, so I was sure Peter was with us in spirit as we celebrated. He would have loved it. He was proud to be Irish, and on St. Patrick's Day in Mazatlan, he wowed the crowd of sailors there with Irish ditties on our marine piano. The Wake was quite a party! Past Commodore Blake Williams had organized a four-piece band – keyboard , fiddle, guitar and *bodhran* (an Irish drum), and they were playing Irish jigs and singing sea shanties. There were song sheets with the words so people could sing along, and when there weren't words we were all up dancing. There were about 50 people there, all my good BCA friends and we all drank a toast to Peter's amazing life. Some of those who attended the wake felt sombre as they climbed the stairs to the venue, thinking it would be a sad evening... until they entered the room and heard the lively music, all in Peter's honour. Everyone had brought food and wine. I had a good time too. That evening, Blake's impromptu musical group decided on the spot to call themselves the "Irish Wakers" and, since then, the name has stuck. They're now a popular Vancouver group that entertains at weddings, parties, festivals and, of course, wakes. (Check them out at www.irishwakers.com.)

Several years later when I was writing this book, Blake told me a story that made me realize how much this Wake impacted those who attended. Apparently during the BCA Peterson Cup Rally around the northern Gulf Islands several years after Peter's death, one of the racers from another boat visited Blake and commented that some time ago he'd attended an Irish Wake that really showed him how the passing of a loved one could be dignified, honourable, and lively. In fact, he said that's how *he* would like to be remembered. Ironically, he was referring to Peter's Wake and did not realize that Blake was one of those in the band. Out of context, perhaps!

Pain and Guilt

Even before the funeral and the wake, at which we were going to celebrate the life of my amazing man, I started to enter the second stage of grief...

> **Stage 2 of Grief – Pain & Guilt:** As the shock wears off, it is replaced with the suffering of unbelievable pain. Although excruciating and almost unbearable, it is important that you experience the pain fully, and not hide it, avoid it or escape from it with alcohol or drugs. You may have guilty feelings or remorse over things you did or didn't do with your loved one. Life feels chaotic and scary during this phase.

Not only did my body ache all over, I couldn't get to sleep - or if I did - I woke up early. I did try a couple of prescription medicines my family doctor gave me, but one was clearly described as being addictive and that thought made me uncomfortable; the second one gave me dizzy spells, so I stopped that one too. However, different people react differently. Sleeping pills may be appropriate for some people. A good night's sleep is important to grieving. It's best to discuss the situation with your doctor.

As an alternative to pharmaceuticals, a friend who had lost her sister very suddenly gave me a small bottle of Rescue Remedy. These are herbal drops that comfort and reassure. She said they were the only thing that helped her to function and to look after her two small children when she was grieving. Rescue Remedy helped me too.

I'd heard that people who have had a leg amputated often can still feel pain in the missing leg, or an itch they can't scratch. Now I understood that. I'd lost half of myself, so no wonder I hurt so much physically. The most helpful thing I discovered was that, if I soaked in a really long hot bath, my body relaxed and the pain disappeared temporarily while I was in the tub. Then, if I quickly dried off and crawled under the covers into bed while my body was still warm, I would almost immediately fall asleep – at least for a couple of hours. I often did this in the middle of the day to make up for the sleep I was losing every night. At this stage, it's physical comfort which helps so much. Be gentle to yourself!

The second stage is not just pain; it also includes guilt. Not only were there things I felt guilty about almost immediately, such as – why had I taken precious seconds to call my daughter Tara and Debbie, an Associate Pastor at her church, before calling 911 to summon an ambulance? Maybe if I had been faster, the doctors could have saved my husband. Other guilty thoughts would haunt me for months and years after Peter's death. I would remember things Peter did that had annoyed me and I'd feel guilty that I'd been annoyed at the time. For example, he would tell jokes and stories over and over again. Peter had a gift for storytelling, and I always laughed the first time I heard one. But whenever he'd start retelling a favourite story to someone new, I'd roll my eyes and ignore it. Now I felt guilty that I'd not supported and encouraged him more in this gift. Today, I would give anything to have him back, telling any of the stories from his vast repertoire. I now realize that we all just do the best we can at the time. Giving ourselves guilt over what we *shoulda, coulda, woulda done* is fruitless.

Peter was more outgoing than I was; he'd spontaneously invite perfect strangers to come aboard *Wanderlust V* for coffee or a beer. I'd groan inwardly, because I always wanted to be the perfect hostess and have the boat tidy and snacks prepared in advance for

---

Ideas for Getting to Sleep
- Stick to a regular schedule.
- Get regular exercise every day, but not within three hours of going to bed.
- Avoid caffeine and alcohol, or at least limit the quantity.
- Eat light at the evening meal.
- Avoid sleeping pills – it's too easy to become dependent.
- Get sunlight in the afternoon.
- Create a sleep-producing atmosphere – low lighting, soothing music, a hot bath, deep breathing, visualization of a beautiful setting, inspirational reading.

---

guests. I was slowly learning to become more spontaneous like him, but after his death I felt guilty that I hadn't more cheerfully and more quickly followed his lead.

It was at this time, in those early empty months following Peter's death, that I remembered the literature the kind social worker at the hospital had given me that included a listing of community resources available to those suffering grief. One such organization was the Surrey Hospice Society, located not far from where I lived. They offered grief therapy sessions at a very minimal cost. I wasn't sure if this would help, but it was worth a try. As the weeks after Peter's death went by, and the family resumed their own lives and necessarily had less time for me, I found I was starting to feel overwhelmed by the thought of living alone for the rest of my life. I missed Peter *so* much. Somewhat to my surprise, I found that the grief therapy group helped a lot. I was not alone. In one of the early sessions I attended, I was given several questions to think about.

Here are the answers I gave:

Q: What do you wish you had done while your loved one was alive?
A: *Listened to him more.*

Q: What did you do that pleases you or makes you proud?
A: *I loved him with all my heart.*

Q: What do you miss the most?
A: *His warm body beside me in bed.*

Q: What do you not miss?
A: *His temper.*

Q: What did you discuss with your loved one that you are glad you talked about?
A: *He gave me a complete description of what was wrong with our car the day before he died. I was then able to repeat that to*

the mechanic, and as a result, he was able to fix it – for long enough that I could sell it in running condition!

Q: What do you think you can never do now?
A: Sail Wanderlust V to the South Pacific.

Q: What can you do that you could not do while your loved one was alive?
A: Play country and western music.

Q: What do you wish your loved one had done?
A: Not smoked.

Q: What did your loved one do that made you happy?
A: Small jobs on the boat like putting a light in the fridge, or sliding drawers in the boat's lockers. He often did these things without telling me, just to surprise and please me.

Q: What new understandings do I now have about my relationship with my loved one?
A: How visible our love for each other was to all our friends.

At the time I felt guilt about some of these answers, but they were honest answers. Since then I've learned so much more – I could give a dozen answers to each question. I don't feel guilt at all and the answers I gave are still very honest.

How Friends and Family Can Help

Of course it's natural that family and friends want desperately to help a person in grief. But they don't always know how or what to say. Meaning well, they respond with platitudes about "closure" or "I understand how you feel, but..." or "There, there, don't cry. Everything will work out. Time will heal your pain." Though they meant well, sometimes I wanted to scream.

> **Time does NOT heal. It's the grieving - crying, talking, journaling and praying that bring healing.**

I've learned that "closure" is just a convenient word for the media to wrap up their stories of grief. What I've come to believe through my own voyage through grief is that, although time does *not* heal, it is possible to learn to live with the hole in your heart and that no one else can ever truly understand how you really feel. It's the grieving itself - crying, talking, journaling and praying – that brings healing. The best thing anyone can say to someone who is grieving is "Grieve well." Or, "I'm so sorry for your loss. May I get you a cup of tea?" Or, just sit beside your friend and hold his or her hand, or offer a tissue and your shoulder to cry on.

However, everyone grieves differently, and if you have any doubts about that, I recommend reading *The Heart Does Break*, compiled by Jean Baird and George Bowering. It contains stories from 19 Canadian authors, ranging from the suicidal to almost merry. The book helped me better appreciate how we all grieve differently, that there is no right or wrong. Sometimes it helps to talk about the loved one and to use his name. For example, "Peter was such a good friend," or "I remember when Peter..." Sharing a special memory with the grieving person about the person who has died is often better than any offer of condolence. And sometimes just being there may be all the support someone needs.

The Elephant in the Room

There is an elephant in the room.
It is large and squatting, so it is hard to get around it.
Yet we squeeze by with, "How are you?" and "I'm fine..."
And a thousand other forms of trivial chatter.
We talk about the weather.
We talk about work.
We talk about everything else
Except the elephant in the room.
There is an elephant in the room.
We all know it is there.
We are thinking about the elephant as we talk.
It is constantly on our minds.
For you see, it is a very big elephant.
But we do not talk about the elephant in the room.
Oh, please, say her name.
Oh, please, say "Barbara" again.
Oh, please, let's talk about the elephant in the room.
For if we talk about her death,
Perhaps we can talk about her life.
Can I say, "Barbara" and not have you look away?
For if you cannot, you are leaving me.
Alone...in a room with an elephant...

(www.missionswithpurpose.com/the-elephant-in-the-room-by-terry-kettering/)

Condolences

In addition to phone calls and personal visits from friends, I treasure all the handwritten cards, letters and the e-mail messages that came flooding in from all around the world. Not only did these messages bring me great comfort, they were further confirmation that there were people all over the world who remembered and would miss my husband. It was similar to what I had experienced at Peter's Celebration of Life Service seeing so many friends from years ago. I was not alone. They were writing to *me* to give me the message that they had not forgotten what a wonderful man Peter was, and that they mourned and sympathized with me. Here are a few:

We will always remember Peter to be a go-getter, a helper, a compassionate man and a very pleasant and comfortable person to be with. Someone who was fun to listen to, both in person and on the radio, with his quick wit. Both of our daughters enjoyed wandering down the dock to spend time with you and Peter. We will always cherish the memories of listening to Peter's piano playing (which he did with great gusto) and sing-alongs. (SV Peregrinata, French Polynesia)

You both have been such a wonderful couple, sharing so much and showing such dedication and obvious affection for each other. We sit here stunned, as no doubt the whole cruising community is, knowing we have lost a friend. (SV Incognita, Galapagos Islands)

I am in shock...tears are flowing down my face as I type this – we are so lucky to have met you both and had such fun times in San Diego – the way you went out of your way to find us and include us in your life – Peter touched so many people with his zest and sense of fun. (SV Solar Driftwood, New Zealand)

When we think of you and Peter, we will always picture big gregarious smiles and feel the warmth of friendship you two always emitted. When we read Peter's last email...we can only smile. Always upbeat. Said Mother Teresa, 'Let no one ever come to you without leaving better and happier. Be

40

the living expression of God's kindness in your face, kindness in your eye, kindness in your smile.' This will be the Peter (and Glenora) we will remember. (SV Tioga, Barcelona, Spain)

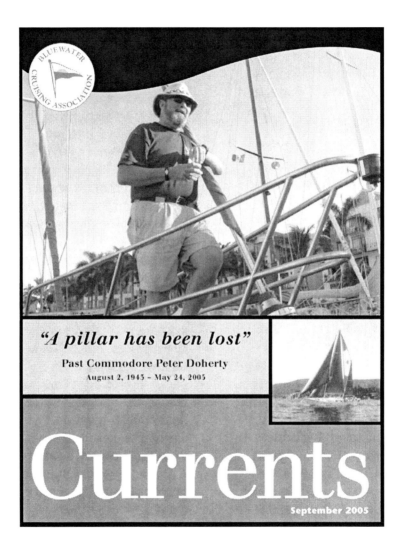

"A pillar has been lost"

Past Commodore Peter Doherty
August 2, 1945 – May 24, 2005

Currents Cover, September 2005

I also treasure the September 2005 issue of *Currents,* which had a photo of Peter on the cover, with the Commodore's caption, "A Pillar has been Lost". Another quote from the "Passages" column in that issue referred to Peter as the "man with a very special sparkle in his eye," and concluded, "I am convinced that if there is a way to go sailing on the other side, Peter will find it. In that very special anchorage, just before sunset, when you are relaxing with a glass of wine in your hand, please look for him. You just may see that special sparkle somewhere on the horizon."

And finally, a card from another military wife and good friend in Ottawa, who had known us for 35 years:

"It was with a mixture of sadness and gladness that we received your letter. The sadness, of course, because of Peter's early demise. You cannot imagine how sad I am of the loss of that wonderful BIG man, BIG heart, BIG temper, BIG intelligence, BIG enthusiasm, BIG dreams. The world is indeed a poorer place

My Journal is My Friend

- My journal offers a ready release. It's always with me in my purse or pocket when I leave the house. My friends are not that available.
- Writing slows me down to a pace I can handle. It gets me off the treadmill of going nowhere.
- Writing helps me separate my jumbled feelings into what is happening in my life.
- If I organize my problems on paper, I can begin to write possible solutions.
- I can always refer back to my journal and check my progress.
- Questions without answers can be written down and left on paper. It stops them from going around and around in my head.
- As my grief is released, I begin to see breaks, I begin to see through the clouds. It feels good.
- A running chronicle gives me a "then" and "now" to measure my growth.
- My journal is proof of my survival.

without him. Just the thought of him brings tears to my eyes. I truly loved him. Gladness because I see by your letter that you have not allowed your loss to beat you. You are still as strong as ever. You will always be a shining example to your family."

These messages served another purpose. At a time when I was unsure who I was, they taught me things about myself. I learned how obvious our love for each other appeared to other people and that our friends saw me as a strong person. Both those things felt good.

Journaling and Letters to Peter

One of the things that helped me most, and still does, is journaling. I had kept a personal diary as a teenager; shortly after Peter and I were married, we started an annual Doherty Journal that we sent to family and friends every Christmas; and I started a daily journal when the boat was launched in 1988. So I already had lots of experience. I'd learned that in times of stress, such as when Peter had his nervous breakdown after his retirement, writing about it took some of the burden off my shoulders and out of my mind. I wouldn't forget it if it was written down, because then I could go back and read it any time. On the other hand, it didn't stay in my mind as a nagging thought. The other benefit was that I could look back and see how far I'd come. I highly recommend journaling. You don't have to be a good writer; you don't even have to write full sentences - just jotting down words or phrases as they come into your mind and dating them serves the purpose.

Another good idea is to keep a gratitude journal. Every day, just write down things you are grateful for; no matter how small or insignificant you think they are. Or even better, use it as a prayer book, to give thanks to God each day for your blessings.

When something exciting or good happened, I naturally wanted to share it with Peter, but he wasn't there to tell, so I developed a special kind of journal – I started writing letters to him. I have about a dozen letters and I've kept them all. Here's my first one to him after he died:

My darling Peter,

You've been gone now for over five months, the longest we've ever been apart. I just want to tell you I love you, I miss you *so* much, and life will never be the same. I am so grateful I had you for as many years as I did - 41 wonderful years of marriage, especially the last 11 that we lived aboard *Wanderlust V*, and the three years since we retired. Yes, I know there were times in the last three years that the adjustment for both of us was tough living together 24/7 with no one else to supervise or give orders to - but we were making it! Despite the ups and downs of Hurricane Marty and flying back and forth for your medical tests, we were living aboard *Wanderlust V* and making her into the beauty we'd always dreamed she would be. I think you and I were closer in the last year than we'd ever been before.

Our kids have been wonderful, taking care of me, loving me, keeping me company, amusing me, worrying me, and reminding me of you. There is so much of you in each of them. When Ryan hugs me, I feel your presence.

I don't know what to do with all your stuff and things—clothing, shoes, marine life statues, office files, books, magazines, etc. Yet there are so many things we left in storage that I'm so enjoying having around me again—our paintings, books, statues, china, silver, and all that incredible teak furniture, especially the wall unit. I have two sections in the dining area, and two more in the living room for the stereo and TV equipment. Right now, I'm sitting at that wonderful teak fold-out desk we bought in California years ago, typing this on *your* laptop – and no, I haven't busted the keyboard yet! (I type so fast I've destroyed at least two keyboards.) However, it's making strange noises when I start it up. It's three years old now.

Do you know that I received hundreds of emails from cruisers all around the world sympathizing with me on your death? And that you were on the front cover of September *Currents*? And that a new BCA award is being created in your memory? It's called the Peter Doherty Goodwill Ambassador Award. Nothing could be more fitting for you.

I wish you could have seen our grandchildren on Halloween night—all four of them went out trick or treating together. The girls were princesses, Matthew was a space ranger and Daryan a pumpkin. What fun! I bought two of the costumes, and shortened Angie's dress. Angie had just arrived from Peru with her Mom three weeks earlier, speaking whole sentences in Spanish, but she learned three new English phrases that night: "Trick or Treat", "Thank you", and "Bye, bye".

Today I helped Jackie fill out her immigration forms. That she is here with Ryan and the kids, and applying to become a permanent resident of Canada is unbelievably wonderful. I guess God meant for them to be here for me after you left.

I got a lovely card from our dentist in Victoria today. He called you the "gentle giant". Your sister Jennifer says she misses her big brother with his bigger than life personality. So many people have referred to your big heart. You were a big guy in so many respects.

Remember the electronic sound mixer that came with all the other electronics in the suitcase accompanying your brother's keyboard, after he died? I donated it to Tara's church and the worship team is using it for their rehearsals. They were most grateful, and I thought both you and David would approve.

I'm bawling my eyes out as I write this. All the books I've read on grief, all the social workers and pastors I've talked to, and the facilitators at the grief support group I attended for six weeks – they all tell me to let it out, cry, bawl, shout, whatever – don't keep it bottled up and suppressed. So I cry. I talk about you a lot to anyone who will listen.

However, I am also learning things about myself. I'm learning that I'm stronger than I ever thought I would be. I'm learning that I can be a bubbly person even when I'm in mourning. I'm learning that I enjoy my solitude and living alone (to a certain extent). I get to make all the decisions now, right or wrong, and to live with the consequences. I have a pink and purple bedroom. I doubt you would ever have stood for that! Even all the blue I love so much overwhelmed you, so you'll believe me when I say that my new car is blue! I've learned to use a screwdriver, how to fill the gas tank, I've written a new will, invested more money, even assembled IKEA furniture from the instructions, and I made a breakfast omelette for the kids one morning - as close to your recipe as I could - and everybody loved it.

I'm back on the BCA Watch in a new position as Archives Watchkeeper, preserving and sharing BCA's fascinating history with members. Again, something I know you'd approve. I've learned how to scan photographs, first for the slide show Tara did for your service, and secondly for old BCA photos I'm publishing in *Currents* and putting up on the website.

I'm sleeping better the last few nights. Our family doctor has me on an anti-depression pill that has the side effect of drowsiness. It takes a couple of weeks to take effect, and I think it just kicked in. Or, I'm actually starting to heal from your loss. I know I will always miss you; but I also think there will come a time when I will experience a full life and joy again – in a different way. I do have a lot to live for – Tara, Brian, T'ea, Matthew, Ryan, Jackie, Angie, Daryan, and kitty Marty. But there's no doubt in my mind I'm going through the biggest challenge I have ever faced in my life. Even coping with your severe depression in 1984-85 pales by comparison to losing you forever. We've lived through so many highs and lows together, but this low I have to face by myself.

I will stop now, but I'll write you again, my darling. G.

A "Peter Day"

I also started allowing myself to have an occasional "Peter Day". It was Peter's sister, Jennifer, who coined this expression for me. Some days when I was feeling lonely and depressed, I would just surrender myself to it. I'd leave the bed unmade, sit around drinking coffee in my dressing gown until the afternoon, re-read condolence cards, look through photo albums that brought back memories of our life together, and cry. Or I'd just do nothing - "veg out" in front of the TV or play a mindless computer game. I told Jennifer I felt guilty about being so lazy and unproductive. She told me it was okay to spend a day feeling sad. Was my time so precious I couldn't afford to give one day to Peter's memory? Of course I could! And here's the funny thing — the day after, I usually felt refreshed and ready to get back to the to-do list of things that needed to be done. Most of my "Peter Days" came during the first year after his death.

Administrative Arrangements After a Death

With the death of a loved one comes paperwork and other arrangements. Copies of Peter's death certificate were necessary for claiming life insurance; changing the title on our car, house and boat; informing his pensions offices; removing his name from our joint bank accounts, credit cards and other financial records. I ordered four copies of his death certificate from the funeral home, knowing that in some cases, I only had to show it to the relevant office rather than give it to them. In order to authorize Peter's autopsy and cremation, I had to provide a copy of Peter's will showing I was his trustee. Making phone calls to inform authorities of his death was emotionally exhausting. It took courage and strength every time I had to say the words, "I'm calling to inform you that Peter Doherty passed away on May 24th..."

Another reality to face, after the funeral is over, was all the administrative items related to wills, estates, taxes, ownership, etc.. It would have been overwhelming had Peter and I not planned ahead. Just as there is always a risk in surgery, there is a similar small risk of death as the result of serious illness, accidents, drowning or sinking of the boat at sea. This is why most cruisers purchase a life raft and prepare a ditch bag with survival gear and provisions.

Advance Preparations for the Death of a Spouse

I believe all couples should take time to plan for each other's death – long before there is even a hint of any serious medical problem. No one knows when illness or an accident may end someone's life. Planning ahead makes it easier for the surviving spouse or family to go on living. Because Peter and I were planning on heading offshore in *Wanderlust V*, we carefully set about taking care of business in 2002 before we cast off from the dock. We

Advance Paperwork Preparation for the Unthinkable

- Consult a recommended financial planner.
- Designate one or more close relative or friend in whom you have absolute trust, as your representative (in our case a land contact) and give that person Power of Attorney (POA) for both of you.
- Review all insurance policies: boat, house, car, medical and life and update as appropriate.
- Create a file that includes account numbers, Social Insurance Numbers, contact information, expiry dates and passwords for all sources of income, credit cards, bank accounts, and insurance policies, and recent tax returns, and leave it with your POA.
- Prepare wills.
- If possible, put all your income into a joint bank account, and give your POA signing authority.
- Make a list of all items left in storage.
- Take out a safety deposit box for original important documents.

didn't want to leave a mess behind for our children to sort out, if we both died at the same time at sea.

We consulted a certified financial planner about the best investments for our RRSPs and the severance packages we both received upon retirement. We chose low-risk, well-diversified mutual funds because we knew we would not be around to monitor these investments ourselves when we were in foreign countries or making offshore passages. Our advisor had our daughter's contact information and our email address in the event he needed to contact us.

We reviewed all our insurance policies (life, car, boat, house, medical) in light of the fact we were heading offshore and made appropriate revisions and arranged for automatic payments from our bank account. We also arranged for all our pension cheques to be automatically deposited. We added our daughter's name to our joint chequing account, so she could write cheques to pay unexpected bills for us in our absence, if necessary.

Questions to ask yourself include:
- Is the amount of insurance sufficient?
- Who has Power of Attorney to claim the benefit in your absence?
- If one of you has an accident or develops a serious illness in a foreign country, do you have sufficient insurance to cover treatment?
- Do you have enough cash to fly back home for medical treatment, if necessary?"

We saw a lawyer and wrote our wills, gave each other Power of Attorney and also to our daughter in the event of our absence or incapacity. The simplest will is to leave everything to each other and to make each other the executor of your estate. This covers the death of one of you. But add whatever clauses are appropriate, in the event that you both die together, outlining your wishes. Paying for professional advice can help ensure that what you wish for your partner and family is actually what happens in the event of your death.

We had registered our wish to donate our organs with the British Columbia Transplant Society. Check their website for information on how to register and how it works: http://www.transplant.bc.ca. However, much to my regret and I'm sure Peter's, his wish to make this kind of a donation wasn't possible because an autopsy had been ordered. All his organs had to stay in place for that purpose, rather than being transplanted immediately to a waiting recipient. We had always owned everything jointly, which I know is becoming a less common practice for couples today; however, it certainly made many arrangements simpler for me to handle. My banker called me as soon as she saw the obituary in the paper, and after extending her condolences, she assured me that I could continue using my bank accounts and my credit card issued by her bank without any problem. All were owned jointly with Peter. She asked me to call her for an appointment whenever I felt ready, to come in with his death certificate to sign papers to pay off our insured line of credit and credit card, and to remove Peter's name from all our joint accounts. I had been warned by friends that our joint bank account could be frozen until probate; she assured me this was not true in my case. (However this can happen if proper planning is not made ahead of time.)

It was also a simple matter to transfer title of the car to me and at the Ship's Registry to transfer title for the boat. All I needed to provide was Peter's death certificate, my photo ID and current registration papers. It took no more than 30 minutes. The house, which we owned jointly with our daughter and son-in-law, was a little more complicated because there were four owners. Peter and I were "tenants in common" owners, and so Peter's share of the house automatically transferred to me when his name was removed from the title. However, the bank that held our mortgage took care of that, again with a copy of the death certificate.

Every couple's circumstances will be different but proper planning will help bring some peace of mind at a time when the surviving partner needs it most.

The house arrangement we had was ideal for an offshore couple. We had a permanent mailing address while we were off cruising, a free storage area (unfinished basement room) for books, photographs, files, winter clothing, furniture, etc., and rental income while we were gone. Tara acted as our property manager, earning a percentage of the rent she collected each month. We also expected that when the time came that we were finished sailing, this is where we would live for at least the first year, until we could decide what we wanted to do and where we wanted to live. And we only very briefly mentioned...*if* one of us were to die or become disabled in any way, we'd have a home right downstairs from our loving daughter. We didn't dwell on that "if" for very long, but it was no coincidence that I had a home waiting for me.

I realize this arrangement wouldn't work for everyone, but I would encourage any couples who travel extensively by land, air or sea to do something similar. At the very least, just *think* about and discuss where you'll live when you return. No one likes to think about what one of us would do if the other died, but we *should* think about it. If you own your own home, think about whether your current home will still be suitable, if one of you dies:

- Will the survivor be able to afford the taxes, mortgage and maintenance costs?
- Could you physically handle the upkeep by yourself?
- Would you want to live there if you were left alone?

Before we left, we gave our daughter our planned itinerary and all the written specifications about the crew and the boat (commonly referred to as a sail plan) which the Coast Guard would need to know if they were searching for us at sea. Then I made a list of all our pension numbers, credit cards, bank accounts, insurance policies, complete with expiry dates, passwords, contact information and put this together in an "Important Documents" file. We left one copy with our daughter, as well as a key to our safety deposit box, and put the original documents, including our wills, in our own bank safety deposit box. All these documents were invaluable to me, when I had to settle Peter's estate.

Steps to Survival – Stage 2

- ❖ Nutrition: Good eating habits help the healing process.
- ❖ Accept support and comforting from others. It's human and courageous.
- ❖ Allow yourself a "day off" occasionally, to cry, reflect and to remember.
- ❖ Keep all your condolence cards and letters; they will comfort you on your "day off".
- ❖ Celebrate special happy occasions like the anniversary of your wedding.
- ❖ Talk about happy memories.
- ❖ Note happy as well as sad thoughts in your journal.
- ❖ It's okay to feel guilt. Be honest with yourself. Don't worry if your guilt sounds illogical. It often is. Express it openly to a trusted friend or a qualified professional.
- ❖ Seek trusted, professional medical advice if you need prescription medications.
- ❖ Take a hot bath to relax before sleep.

3
Challenges

God grant me the serenity to accept the things I cannot change...
The courage to change the things I can
And the wisdom to know the difference.
(St. Francis of Assisi)

When you are grieving the death of someone you love, there are many challenges you will have to deal with - including anger, returning to emotionally sensitive rooms or places, moving to a new home, unpleasant memories, disposing of personal effects, dealing with special dates and times of the year, perhaps even experiencing visitations from the deceased, losing one's identity, adjusting to a changed marital status, problem solving alone, and maintaining good nutrition. To a greater or lesser extent, I experienced all of these challenges. And I learned how to cope with each one of them and then to move forward.

Anger

For some who are grieving, their anger towards God, the doctors, the medical system, or even the loved one who is gone, can be searing and very real. This is the third stage of grief.

> **Stage 3 of Grief – Anger & Bargaining:** Frustration gives way to anger, and you may lash out and lay unwarranted blame for the death on someone else. Please try to control this, as permanent damage to your relationships may result. This is a time for the release of bottled up emotion. You may rail against fate, questioning "Why me?" You may also try to bargain in vain with the powers that be, for a way out of your despair, for example, "I will never drink again if you just bring him back."

As children, we're taught that it's not nice to be angry and that we shouldn't admit to or express our anger. However, angry feelings are a normal and a healthy response to loss. It is especially difficult to admit being angry with the sick or dead person, e.g. for abandoning you and for getting sick. You may be angry with God for not answering your prayers or for the unfairness of it all. "He was such a good person, why did God have to take him? It's not fair!"

Not everyone expresses their anger outwardly. Some people don't kick or scream or beat pillows. But that doesn't mean they aren't in the grip of this powerful emotion. Anger can be subtle and even subconscious; the fact that I had trouble sleeping may have been a result of inner anger that I didn't want to acknowledge. Or, we are fearful of anger because we're afraid that expressing it may damage our relationship with the one we blame.

However, anger is an emotion. And it's a *healthy* emotion. It's an internal signal telling us about something we don't like. Anger is meant to be *acted on*. It's a call for action. If it's not acted on and, instead, is turned inward, it may contribute to depression. Many of us are more comfortable becoming depressed than allowing ourselves to become angry.

Sometimes we experience frozen anger or rage. If you deny it, bury it, block it, hide it, lie about it – do anything but listen to it - it will smoulder inside you and eventually poison you. Chronic headaches, backaches, earaches and sinus problems can be indications that you are holding unexpressed anger. It may also be a factor in such physical conditions as ulcers, arthritis, colitis, high blood pressure or constipation. So although it's important to let it out, I suggest you take out your anger on things, not people!

I don't recall feeling anger about Peter's death; after all, there are only two things certain in life: death and taxes. Who would I blame? Some people blame the doctors for not doing enough or God for letting it happen. The way I see it, death is a natural part of life. We all die some day. However, I did feel frustrated, annoyed, disappointed, upset, and surprised. These are other words people sometimes use to talk about anger without actually saying, "I'm angry" - so perhaps I was more angry than I was prepared to admit, even to myself.

The closest I came to an outburst of anger was when I eventually returned to *Wanderlust V* in Mexico and started taking stock of all the "stuff" on board. Peter was by nature a pack rat. He never liked to get rid of anything. He had every tool on the boat that had been used to build her, except the table saw - no space aboard for that! For example, he carried around a spare two square foot piece of Plexiglas that he had bought – and never used - when we started the construction of the boat in 1980. Even when we left for offshore in 1989 and again in 2002, that same piece of Plexiglas was stowed under the cushions of one of the berths with all the other scraps of spare lumber. It was an area our family affectionately called the "lumber yard". Though sometimes an irritation, I understood the need for us to be prepared for anything when we ventured offshore. In 2002 we encountered some very rough weather sailing from San Diego to Turtle Bay, Mexico. One of the lines in the mainsheet caught the windshield wiper, causing the mainsheet block (a set of pulleys) to collide with the centre panel of the windshield, shattering it with a bang! The windshield had been custom built for us in Vancouver many years before, and getting a replacement would have been next to impossible in Mexico. Yet as soon as we were safe in harbour and anchored, out came the Plexiglas and Peter cut it to size. (Of course we had a hardware store of tools, adhesives and fasteners aboard - everything we needed for the job.) Presto! A new windshield. Peter didn't say, "I told you so." He didn't need to.

However, after his death, the job of disposing of all those spare parts, tools and supplies on the boat became my responsibility when I was back in Mazatlan. Faced with these reminders of Peter's care and diligence, reminders of 29,000 wonderful miles sailing together, and the sheer amount of stuff to dispose of, my frustrations boiled into anger with Peter himself...

> This afternoon, in the midst of emptying and combining lockers on the boat, I started emptying the "office" locker and burst into tears. I found at least 15 pairs of sunglasses, several reams of paper, two large bags of elastic bands, 6 rolls of scotch tape,

and a whole shoe box of pens and pencils. And in the head (bathroom), I emptied the cabinet of lotions and creams Peter had cleared out from his aunt's room when she had died several years earlier. I'm overwhelmed by all this stuff on this boat – it's stocked as if we weren't going to see land again for five years. How could Peter leave me with this mess to deal with? (Journal, February 7, 2006)

I felt really angry and overwhelmed and burst into tears. I moaned "Oh, no!" and after a few minutes, with shaking hands, I shoved most of the stuff back in the locker to deal with another day. The half-used lotions and creams went into the garbage. For hours afterwards, I felt miserable with guilt for feeling angry. And most of the stuff in the "office" didn't get cleared out for many more months – until I was back in Canada and could put this in the perspective of just being another to-do job.

I also know Peter's 89-year-old mother was angry at God for taking her son. She had a lot to be angry about. Her second son, David, had died suddenly just a few short months before Peter. She was facing the fact that she had outlived both her sons, whom she adored. I remember holding her in my arms in Calgary as she sobbed over the loss of David. It was the first time in the 45 years I had known her that I had ever seen her cry. She was so devastated that she couldn't even bear to attend David's funeral, although she did view his body in the funeral home and said he looked "at peace". Mom Doherty is a strong, beautiful lady who always thought the best of everyone. She loves people and she loves life. When she was 74, she sailed with us aboard *Wanderlust V* from Sitka, Alaska, to Prince Rupert, BC, an 18-day trip. She came to Vancouver for Peter's service, and even got up at the microphone at the reception to speak well of all her "boys" (Peter, David and her late husband), now up in heaven. She's a survivor, who is still a loving, gracious and courageous lady today at age 95.

My son was also angry - or maybe it was more frustrated, disappointed or shocked. Although he told me he cried in Peru after Tara called him with the shocking news, from the time he arrived in

Canada for his dad's service, he never shed a tear. I know without a doubt how much he loved his father and what a shock and trauma it was for him to lose Peter. Perhaps part of his anger, disappointment and frustration came from the fact that just as he and his dad were starting to become adult friends and his dad was starting to recognize his son and give him credit for all his talents and abilities, his dad went and died on him. Ryan never got a chance to fully enjoy that new relationship, let alone the opportunity to say goodbye to him. Ryan had dreams of working with his father, the engineer, on community building projects in Peru, and when we got old, to come to help us to sail *Wanderlust V*. Peter's death shattered these dreams for him.

Peter and *his* father had had a similar relationship, but a few weeks before his Dad died, Peter had had an opportunity to really talk to him one-on-one. They both came out of that chat knowing they'd resolved any outstanding differences and said their goodbyes with love and admiration for each other.

I know Peter expected a lot from Ryan as a child, and I often felt caught in the middle between these two men in my life. I loved them both unconditionally, but I sensed and understood the tension between them. When Ryan was born, there couldn't have been a prouder father. Peter's first born was a *son!* And sons are meant to follow in their father's footsteps, aren't they? But Ryan didn't. As he was growing up, he always wanted to do things differently. He basically ran away from home at 17 to make his own way in the world – the hard way. I've often joked that it was all due to his breech birth. He'd tried to come into the world backwards and has been doing everything the hard way ever since!

It's amazing, though, how smart a dad suddenly becomes when the child becomes a man. All the members of our family remember how Peter taught us to coil a line on *Wanderlust V*. It was simple once we learned, but it was complicated – doubling the line, winding it into a figure of eight by stretching arms straight out in front of you and then pulling the last loop through one end of the coil to hang it up on a hook. Peter always insisted we all do it the same way, because lines coiled consistently the same way made for quicker and safer use. My daughter Tara and I grumbled good naturedly about this, but Ryan argued about it. Peter told him that if he had his own boat one day, he could do it his own way, "Different skippers, different long splices." Then one day a few years after Ryan had left home and was living on his own, Peter and I were taking a troop of Sea Scouts out sailing for the weekend and Peter invited Ryan to join us and help out with the boys. Before we left the dock, I happened to notice Ryan up on the foredeck, showing a couple of the boys how to coil a line — his dad's way!

Perhaps anger can be such a challenge to live with because we are trained so well not to admit it and because being angry at the person who died so often feels like disloyalty. Yet anger is an emotion as natural as any other, including love. When anger overwhelms, I believe our challenge is not to flee but to try to accept it and to work through it. In my own experience, I've found that the anger eventually recedes, and we are wiser having had the experience.

Certain Words, Phrases, Rooms or Places

Certain words or phrases can create some very unpleasant reactions. The first time a dear friend of mine, who had also lost her husband years earlier, referred to me as a "widow" I absolutely cringed. For me it had connotations of being old, boring, poor, lame, and a maybe a bit eccentric. I didn't want to be a widow, but I didn't have much choice when it came to filling out income tax forms or other financial documents. It took time to feel more comfortable with the notion of being a widow.

Certain rooms or places become a challenge when you need to protect yourself from additional stress, especially when you fear your response to the place may be too intense for you to handle. For some people who have lost a child, they never have enough strength or courage to remove or change anything in their child's bedroom. The last place their child slept, his favourite things, his clothes and personal belongings remain untouched because, perhaps for years, entering the room is much too painful.

Going back to *Wanderlust V* in Mexico was like that for me. She alone held all the best memories of my life with Peter. The thought of returning, of being aboard her without my skipper scared me. For months, I put off even thinking about it. However, feelings of responsibility for the boat I loved so much finally won out. I think I even felt some guilt because I knew Peter would expect me to take good care of her.

The challenge for me was softened by a kind offer from my good friends, Barbara Angel and Ian Monsarrat, to come with me because they'd said they'd love to get away in the winter and spend a couple of months on a sailboat in sunny Mexico! This was as good as it was going to get and I knew I couldn't delay any longer.

We flew to Mazatlan eight months after Peter's death. When we walked down the dock at El Cid Marina, the sight of my beautiful *Wanderlust V* lying there waiting for me actually brought tears of joy to my eyes. Her hull was gleaming and showed off her beautiful sleek lines. It was like seeing an old friend I hadn't seen in a long time. However, as soon as I got closer, I saw the doubled up

"When a lady's husband dies, why does she hafta be a window?"

59

mooring lines, which Peter had used all his strength to tighten just before we left, in preparation for the hurricane season and for the well-known surge that can sweep into that particular marina.

When I stepped below into the interior, everything I saw reminded me of Peter. There was the special bronze hook he'd installed on the companionway door to make it easier for my small fingers to open it; his spare Tilley hat hanging on a hook just inside the entrance where he'd left it, the gleaming edge of the main bulkhead that he'd just finished laminating and varnishing a few months before, and a list of "to do on return to the boat" items in his own handwriting on the chart table.

I think going aboard the boat that day was the hardest, most courageous thing I did in my entire voyage through grief. Even on the plane as we circled to land in Mazatlan, I had knots of apprehension in my stomach. When I saw all these reminders aboard, I felt numb, dazed, overwhelmed and aching with loneliness for Peter. It wasn't right that he wasn't there!

Every action of daily living while I was there continued to remind me of him. Although I continued to sleep in the double berth in the bow of the boat where I had always slept, the other side was very empty and cold. Peter wasn't there to play the piano as I cooked or cleaned in the galley. Around the marina, I had to face other cruisers who were seeing me for the first time after Peter's death. At first, they didn't know how to relate to me without him or what to say. (I discovered quickly, though, that a hug was all we both needed.) And the first time I sailed *Wanderlust V* without him and enjoyed feeling the wind and sun on my face and her gentle movement, it was heartbreaking to realize that we would never again share that joy together. "Our" dream had ended.

However, I had my friend Barb to hug me and give me a shoulder to cry on—not only on that first day, but often during our stay aboard while we cleaned, inspected equipment, sorted through lockers, ate, slept, and socialized – either up at the pool or out to dinner with other cruisers.

Bringing the Boat Home

I can imagine that others who lose their husband or wife may have the challenge of moving to a new home after their spouse dies, because the old home is too expensive or too difficult for one person to maintain. In my case I had to move my home from one country to another, which involved a most complicated series of logistical and financial arrangements.

I returned to Mazatlan, Mexico, in April 2006 to start the process of sailing *Wanderlust V* from Mazatlan to La Paz, waiting there for the Dockwise Yacht Transport ship to arrive, loading her on Dockwise, spending the night on a friend's boat and returning to Canada by air the next day. Ten days later, I would be taking a ferry across to Nanaimo on Vancouver Island to take delivery of *Wanderlust V*, spend one night at a marina there, and sail her back to a new marina in Vancouver.

Before I even returned to Mazatlan, I was busy making numerous long distance international phone calls, sending regular emails back and forth to Dockwise, completing customs declarations, requesting under body measurements and drawings of *Wanderlust V* from the original builder that had to be faxed to Dockwise so they could custom design the steel supports that would be used underway, and arranging for a certified cheque for payment that involved converting currencies. The Dockwise fee was US $11,000 but on top of that there was insurance and moorage costs, and my own airfare.

Why didn't I just sail the boat home? Simple answer: time and money. I'd need crew, and depending on the weather, it could easily take three months - slogging north is not nearly as easy as heading south! And, if I'd blown out a sail en route – and our sails were 17 years old at this point – replacement would have cost me even more than the cost of shipping.

The first physical challenge when I arrived in Mazatlan was sailing her from there to La Paz, 350 miles across the Sea of Cortes. A couple of good BCA friends had offered to crew for me. This crossing would be my fourth crossing of the Sea of Cortes on *Wanderlust V* but the first without Peter. It was definitely the worst. Everything that could go wrong did. In rough, tossing seas – in the dark of night of course – the head (toilet) backed up and I was the one down below cleaning it up. Fortunately, I rarely if ever get seasick or nauseated; apparently I had a stronger stomach than my crew. Secondly, a turning block broke. That's a pulley through which the lines run from the sails to the cockpit and without it, the sail and the line were both flailing and whipping around madly in the dark. And finally, the diesel in our fuel tanks had been sitting for nearly a year and grunge had formed on the bottom of the tank. With the boat tossing about in heavy seas, the fuel got a good stir and we had to change fuel filters three times during our 350-mile passage. However, we arrived safely in La Paz with the same number of crew that had left Mazatlan, which was the criterion Peter and I had always used to define a successful voyage!

The Dockwise schedule is not very precise, so I planned to arrive early and did. Of course that meant it was inevitable that Dockwise would arrive late. I needed to book moorage at a marina (cheaper by the month than day to day, but I didn't know if I'd be there five days or five weeks). I also had to wait until the last minute to book my own flight back to Canada through a Mexican travel agent, because I didn't know for sure when the Dockwise ship would arrive and of course that meant I paid more and had the stress of not knowing when I was leaving. And to make matters worse, while I was there I got an email from Tara to phone her (because of course she couldn't phone me on a boat in Mexico) and she told me that a sewer main had burst and my basement suite that I'd just moved into was flooded with raw sewage. A restoration company and our house insurance took care of it, but the situation still created a lot of stress for me – and for Tara and family upstairs!

The time in La Paz was emotionally difficult too because I had to live alone aboard *Wanderlust V* in a marina for over a month while I waited. That was a new experience. I didn't have Barb's shoulder to cry on and I was surrounded by so many happy and intimate memories that the days were not easy. I made sure to keep myself busy. I did some small boat repairs, swam in the pool every afternoon, shopped, went sightseeing, and renewed acquaintances in a city where I'd previously lived for over a year. There were several BCA cruisers in La Paz at that time, and some were at the same marina as me. They all were very kind to include me in any potlucks or gatherings. I also listened to the daily cruisers net on the VHF radio every morning, and said yes to every social opportunity or event that was announced. Furthermore, La Paz is a lovely non-touristy Mexican town. The people are friendly, it was warm and sunny, and I did enjoy my time there, knowing it was probably the last time I'd see Mexico, at least from the deck of a sailboat.

Unpleasant Memories

Particularly in the early days of grief, and amid all the circumstances surrounding the death of your loved one, unpleasant memories about the person who has gone will most likely come flooding back. These may range from remembering arguments or incidents that you regret, to thinking badly of the person and a heightened awareness of their faults or remembering specific scenes just before or after the death.

For me, one of the most powerful unpleasant memories came flooding up from years before, from the days after Peter retired from the military in 1984. We made a very quick move from Greenwood, Nova Scotia, on Canada's Atlantic Coast to Vancouver, BC, on the Pacific coast, after he received an unexpected but attractive offer of employment from a commercial airline.

However, moving into civilian life (in the military we refer to that as "civvy street") proved to be an extremely hard adjustment for Peter. First, the unwritten operating rules for employees in a corporation were very different than in the military. Everybody wore suits, not uniforms with stripes on their shoulders that indicated rank. Secondly, Peter was a perfectionist who wanted to do his best to succeed, but had no experience or understanding of the politics involved in climbing the corporate ladder on civvy street. Thirdly, we were living in a big house in a big city suburb, rather than in married quarters on a military base in a small town. As a couple, we no longer had an officer's mess to provide an automatic social life and we missed our usual network of friends. All of these conditions were factors in creating horrendous stress.

The breaking point for Peter came with new and different work priorities that challenged his integrity. In the military, personnel safety on an aircraft was of paramount importance, but the commercial airline's priority was to sell seats and make a profit. As the airline's Engineering Manager, Peter discovered the cost-saving maintenance shortcuts that they took, but he was powerless to do anything at the risk of losing his new, highly paid job. We lived near the airport in Richmond, and he had nightmares about his company's planes crashing into our own roof or our neighbours' roofs during the night. This combination of stressors resulted in Peter entering into a period of acute depression and severe anxiety, climaxing in an attempted suicide. He was hospitalized for several weeks.

I give the above real-life example to illustrate how drastically life changes can create stress and depression. Fortunately, during Peter's severe depression my own stress never reached such a serious level. But that anxious and wearying time was part of my memories and, with all the changes I was going through after his death, it scared me. I was afraid that if stress built up too much, the same thing could happen to me.

Talking is probably the single most important thing you can do to help yourself heal. I talked about Peter every opportunity I had and to whoever would listen, even though I often sensed my friends' reluctance to do so. I loved it when someone else would tell me a story about Peter or tell me something he'd said to them, that I didn't know. I think friends avoided talking about Peter to me, because they thought it would make me cry.

Dr. Marvin Johnson calls the telling about your person's death, how you feel, what has happened, 'Framing':

Framing

Someone said, "Anything can be borne if a story can be told" Telling your story is healing.

As you tell what happened and how you felt over and over, you'll notice some changes:

- Your story gets briefer, more concise.
- You begin to highlight the main details.
- Your feelings become clearer, easier to handle.
- Meaning slowly, gently begins to surface.

It's as if you've made a picture of your story. All the paragraphs are in place. The commas are where they should be. There's a beginning, a middle and an end.

Finally, after you've told it enough, you can hang your story on the wall. It's framed with your tears. It can stay on the wall of your life and you can look at it whenever you want. You can take it down and handle it. Show it to other people. The important thing is you'll always have it, but you don't have to carry it around with you all the time."

("Framing" printed with permission from Joy and Dr. Marvin Johnson, Centering Corporation, www.centering.org)

When you don't have people around to talk to and you're alone, try to get involved in some sort of activity—reading, embroidery, wood carving, writing, cleaning out cupboards, etc. – basically anything to occupy your mind in a productive way. But don't fall into the trap I did - when I felt lonely or had nothing to do, I often went shopping at a mall where I could be with people. I think there are better ways to spend your time and money. I wound up buying a lot of things I didn't need or want!

I knew I needed time to figure things out. Of course, I was fortunate to have family living upstairs in my house. Even though Brian and the kids were gone to work and school during the day, Tara continued to work from home or part-time for the first few years after Peter's death, and she was usually there when I needed her. Being so close to family was literally a blessing when bad memories came calling.

I recognize that family and friends also have their own lives and that however much they may want to be supportive, they cannot be available all the time. However, I would encourage you to also reach out to other people when you need support. People want to help and they want you to ask them to help. Give them the opportunity to do so when you really need it.

Disposing of Personal Effects

Disposing of your loved one's personal effects is definitely something that should not be rushed but done in your own time. I managed through sheer determination and a lot of tears to deal with all of Peter's clothing and personal effects on the boat, eight months after his death. But it was another year before I was able to clear out all his clothing hanging in the storage room at home. I donated most of it to charity. I had hoped to give some clothes to a friend of his who was the same height and build, but that friend took Peter's death so hard he couldn't bear even to come and look at Peter's clothing. Finally, just before I moved to my new home in 2010, I managed to clear out all the personal items that were still in Peter's teak highboy in my spare bedroom. I asked Ryan and Tara to have a look at what was there - hats, sweaters, t-shirts, belts - and to help themselves. Each of them chose a sweater and a few other small items. Peter had been gone for over five years by this point, but when Tara held her Dad's knitted cardigan to her face, she burst into tears - because it still had his scent, probably because it had been kept folded up in a closed cabinet.

Some of the household items that I moved from the boat to my home (a card file of recipes, some books, my hand mixer) still smell like the boat (a combination of diesel, mildew, and disinfectant) and every time I use them, the smell reminds me of happy days aboard *Wanderlust V.*

I still have one box stored in my garage that has some of Peter's small items which I feel I should keep—his military medals and hats, the slide rule he used in university, and his cuff links, tie tacks and other miscellaneous jewellery. A friend of mine who is also a widow advised me to keep small personal items like this because when my grandchildren grow up, they may appreciate receiving a small gift that once belonged to their Poppa. In the meantime, Ryan has Peter's RCAF ring. Tara has his engineering ring. I had his wedding ring; yes, that's correct - *had*.

In the course of our marriage Peter had three wedding rings. The first was stolen about 16 years after our wedding, when our home in California was broken into. Peter wasn't wearing it because of safety regulations on the shop floor at work. I gave him the second on our 25th anniversary, when we renewed our vows. It slipped off his finger in the swimming pool at Mazatlan after he'd lost weight. His third was a 41st anniversary gift he only wore for six days before he died. Within six months, I was the one who lost it. It was too big for my thumb and one day it just fell off. Somehow that was not traumatic; it actually felt appropriate and "right" that it had disappeared like all the others.

What do other widows do about wearing their own wedding rings? At first I couldn't bear to take mine off. I had three: a solitaire engagement ring, a plain gold wedding band, and a wider 25th anniversary ring decorated with white gold starbursts. The latter we had decided would be embellished with a row of diamonds when we celebrated our 50th. A couple of years later, when loneliness started to set in, I started thinking about the possibility of finding a new husband, or at least a male friend and companion. Peter and I had actually discussed this more than once and we had encouraged each other to remarry if one of us predeceased the other. We believed that those who remarry fairly soon after the death of a long-time spouse, do so *because* they had such a happy successful marriage and they want to recreate that relationship and lifestyle again. It's actually a compliment and praise to the one who died.

When I went off on a cruise with my sister-in-law in 2007, I decided to leave my wedding rings at home in a safe place. If I took them off on the ship, I might lose them or have them stolen. I also decided not to wear them because it might discourage men I met along the way from pursuing a serious friendship with me. All the time I was gone, however, I missed wearing those rings.

A year or so later, after a great deal of thought, I did what my mother had done after my dad died - I had my own wedding rings melted down into a completely new design, which I wear on my right hand. I know their significance and so does my family and very close friends, but to a perfect stranger, I am not wearing a wedding ring on my left hand. Accepting that I am single was hard at first and was certainly driven home every time I tried to book travel arrangements and had to pay an extra single supplement because I was travelling alone.

In my bank safety deposit box I have two more of Peter's rings that are not only valuable, but have a great deal of sentimental value. I am keeping them as gifts for our two grandsons for a special occasion, such as graduation or a wedding. One is a black Alaska diamond ring that belonged to my father and which my mother gave to Peter when my father died, shortly after our marriage. The other is a diamond solitaire ring I gave Peter on our 20th anniversary. I remember him thrusting his hand out to show it to friends and saying, "I'm engaged!" in a suitably high pitched voice, imitating what a newly engaged, excited young lady might do.

And finally, to this day, I still have his red velour dressing gown hanging in my bedroom closet. I don't pull it out very often anymore, but when I do wrap it around me, I can feel his strong arms around me and his love. My eyes smart with tears and I get a big lump in my throat. I don't think of this as something sad; it's a comforting remembrance to feel his presence. I keep his dressing gown to feel close to him.

Another idea related to personal effects, which I thought about briefly - but didn't pursue - was making a patchwork quilt out of Peter's clothing. Another widow in my grief therapy group, who had a ten-year-old son, was making him a patchwork quilt out of his father's clothing which he could keep on his bed every night. I thought this was a lovely idea that would be so comforting, especially to a child.

Special Times of the Year and Memorials

Invariably a surviving spouse is faced with special dates, "firsts" and special times of the year - the first birthday, anniversary, Christmas, etc. without him or her there. Tara's birthday was just four days after Peter died. It was not a happy birthday, because he'd always made the day special for her. Then Father's Day came only a week after his service. Tara told me she still bought him a Father's Day card that year.

Ryan's Tattoo

However, memorials are good. On what would have been Peter's 62nd birthday, a few months after his death, Tara suggested we plant a tree in our back yard in his memory. It was a Japanese pear tree, which everyone in our family affectionately refers to as the Poppa Tree.

Ryan carries a permanent memorial to his dad with him 24 hours a day. He had the Doherty family crest tattooed on his right

69

shoulder, in five colours. The Latin inscription at the top says "Never Forget" and the bottom scroll shows the years of Peter's life, 1943 to 2005.

BCA named an award in memory of my husband, called the Peter Doherty Goodwill Ambassador Award. Other examples of appropriate memorials are the park bench dedicated to the memory of Peter's father, Douglas Doherty, which sits facing the Bow River in Calgary, only a short walk from the house where Peter was born. Another friend I know planted a memorial garden in honour of her husband in the cemetery where he is buried.

Rituals, or "little ceremonies", help us through the painful transitions from life as it was before a death to what it is becoming after the death. One example is wearing something that belonged to Peter. Ryan often wears his dad's Tilley hat. I think of my deceased mother every time I wear a jacket that belonged to her. When I use Peter's tools or play his piano, I remember him.

"When words are inadequate, have a ritual."
(Anon.)

Another ritual is making memory meals. I often make "Peter's Not-Yet-World-Famous Omelette" that he so often made when we invited people to come to our boat for breakfast. It always has eggs, but the other ingredients change depending on what leftovers are in the fridge! Our family has also enjoyed Roast Duck a l'Orange stuffed with wild rice more than once after Peter's death; it was one of his favourite meals. Whenever I'd ask him what he wanted for dinner, you could bet that he'd smile a silly smile and say, "Duck under glass, of course!" One time the kids put an inverted drinking glass on top of the roast duck just to make him laugh.

On my first birthday without him, I was back in Mexico. I bought myself a purple (taconite) and turquoise (Australian opal) ring and said to myself, "This is a birthday gift to me from Peter." He always enjoyed buying pretty things for me, so I knew he'd approve. Also, I reasoned, I was receiving part of his pension income as his surviving spouse; I was just spending *his* money on me, not my own. I vowed that on my birthday every year, I'd pick out a gift from Peter. On one of my significant birthdays without him, I took an eight-week cruise around South America - what a good excuse to spoil myself!

Of course I missed him intensely on the first Christmas after he was gone, but I had all four of my grandchildren with me for the first time, as well as Ryan, Jackie, Tara and Brian. It was hard to be too sad with excited little ones running around on Christmas morning.

I think the important thing is to not let any special occasion or day just happen, but to plan for it in some way. However, I have never marked the day Peter died; well-meaning friends who called or sent me emails remembering him on that day were thinking of me and I appreciated that, but it's not a day I wish to remember. I want to remember him on the special, happy days of his life—like the day he was born or the day we were married - not the sad day of his death!

Visitations

Some people have visitations, that is, they find that they hear, see or feel the presence of the person who has died. This may be comforting or it may present a challenge. Why visitations happen is not important, nor do they need to be explained. Others may find it hard to believe, but when it happens to you, you know what you have experienced. I do know with certainty that I've heard God's voice, felt His calming presence and His nudges to do certain things.

I have a dear friend that I've known for over 40 years who has a special sense of such things, similar to a psychic. She asked me if I ever felt or saw Peter's presence, or heard his voice. She told me that he had visited her in her family room. He was sitting there – wearing his Tilley hat, shirt and pants – on the raised hearth that runs in front of and beside a brick fireplace. She told me not to try to see or hear him, but if it happened, I would know. The only thing I noticed soon after his death was the frequency of hot baths I was having and how soothing they were. After so many years of living on a boat and not having a bath tub aboard, I had come to prefer showering. Whenever we came back to Canada to visit our family or friends who lived in houses, Peter never ever missed the opportunity to have a hot bath; he loved it. I didn't usually bother; I just showered as usual — until after his death. So I wondered, was I getting a message from him about how to relieve my pain? Was he watching over me? Was he telling me how to relax?

When I returned to *Wanderlust V* with friends Barb and Ian, one of the questions that seemed to come up regularly was, "Now I wonder where Peter would have put the tool, gadget, hinge, etc.?" We'd look everywhere in lockers, drawers or tool bags, only to find it sitting in plain view. I discussed many of these "coincidences" via email with my long-time friend, and it made me wonder, was Peter's spirit overseeing and directing all our tasks to restore the boat?

About two years after Peter's death, I attended a weekend women's spiritual retreat with over 20 other women from New Beginnings Community Church. A special feature of this retreat was a period of silence after dinner on Saturday night until after lunch on Sunday. During this silence, we were encouraged to pray silently, read some suggested scriptures, write in our journals, express creativity by painting, or go for walks in the surrounding forest and along the nearby streams, to enjoy the wonder and beauty of all God had created. I retreated to my room to read and write. Instead, I fell asleep. During my nap, Peter appeared in front of me, for the first time since his death. He was coming up the companionway stairs on the boat, smiling directly at me with his eyes twinkling, and wearing his bulky white pullover sweater, my favourite. All I remember is shouting happily, "Oh, Peter! Peter!" Then I woke. I rarely dream, but that day I did. As I have been writing this book and reading my journals, I have been having more dreams in which Peter appears. I can't will myself to dream about him, but I can tell you that when it happens, I always wake up with a smile on my face.

Loss of Identity

Even as I write this book, I am still figuring out who I am without my husband. I had been half of "Peter and Glenora" for over 40 years. Suddenly I was only Glenora again. Who was I without Peter? I had to find myself and to get to know *me* all over again, or else I didn't know what I was going to do with my life. It was in working through other challenges that I've come to realize some of my own strengths and abilities that perhaps I had not been so aware of before. It's a process that has taken me years, but I have certainly come to know a lot more about myself than I did at the time Peter died.

One of the neat things I did after Peter's death was to research my unusual name. Glenora is actually a made-up name. My parents loved the name Lenora, but apparently my dad had a burst of creativity and decided to put a "G" on the front of it, because our last name (my maiden name) was Gamey. Glenora Gamey was a nice alliteration. As a teenager, my future in-laws affectionately called me GG. But over the years I kept wondering if I would ever meet anyone with the same name. (I didn't until my first grandchild, T'ea Glenora Dong, was born!) I even did map searches to find places named Glenora – and there are quite a few. A couple of years ago, I took a road trip up Vancouver Island, primarily to visit friends and relatives, but I'd heard there was a Glenora community west of Duncan, British Columbia. Sure enough, there was a Glenora Store, a Glenora Community Centre, a Glenora Farm, and even a winery that sold Glenora Champagne. Picking up a brochure at the store, I learned that Glenora means "golden valley" in Scotland. That's what that part of Vancouver Island actually looks like – a golden valley. I love it!

In my case, as well as losing my identity as half of "Peter and Glenora", I also faced the challenge of losing my identity as a cruising sailor and the lifestyle that goes with it. And later, when I finally sold the boat, I also feared losing my identity as "Wanderlust". Like other offshore cruisers we met while cruising, I often didn't remember their last names; sometimes I even forgot their first names – but I never forgot a boat name. Peter and I were the "Wanderlusts" not the "Dohertys" to our cruising friends. When he passed away, I still owned the boat and for several years stayed involved sailing in Mexico and in British Columbia. But when the time finally came to sell her, part of me wondered, "How can I do this? Who will I be when I no longer have a boat?" I *am* 'Wanderlust'". As if losing my husband and my lifestyle weren't bad enough, now I was going to lose my boat identity too.

Somehow, I've managed to keep my cruising identity alive. As Commodore of BCA, I wrote a regular column in our monthly magazine, *Currents,* and I often chose to write stories about our previous adventures on *Wanderlust V.* And the new owners of *Wanderlust V* chose to keep the name too; *Wanderlust V* is still out there, sailing on blue water. I've kept the license plate on my car, 1-DRLST. My sole proprietorship, under which I track my revenues and expenses from writing, is called W5 Communications (a double meaning combining the acronym for *Wanderlust V* and the *what, when, where, why* and *who* of a good story or communications.) And I call my home, "Wanderer's Rest". All these may sound like small things, but together they preserve my way of life – wandering through it – and the familiarity of those small things has given me comfort and helped ease my adjustment to my new life.

Change of Marital Status

Accepting my single status meant that my social life changed too and this was another challenge. Fortunately, it didn't seem to make any difference to my cruising friends. I've always felt comfortable as a single woman in social gatherings with other sailors. That's probably because in the cruising community there are men and women who sail singlehanded, couples who are together and then they're not; or couples where only one partner does the offshore passages (with other crew) and the spouse flies to ports to meet the boat and enjoys living aboard in a marina while visiting a foreign country. However, invitations to join other couples – former colleagues, neighbours or ex-military friends - for dinner or an outing were few and far between. At first I heard from many couples with notes and cards of condolence. But I didn't get many invitations to dinner or movies; I'd be a fifth wheel. Within a year, I realized much of my social life had become one of lunches or movies out with the "girls". I've found this hard, because I enjoy talking with men about politics, economics, and sailing just as much as I enjoy chatting with other women about home decorating, clothing, and recipes.

Problem Solving Alone

Making decisions alone was a new experience for me. Peter and I had always worked through difficult situations and solved problems together. Now I had to make my own decisions about where to live, whether to buy a car, how to manage my income and investments, and the hardest decision of all, what to do about the boat. Sometimes it took me a long time to figure out what was the best course of action, but gradually the process has become easier.

I deliberately took my time in making the more significant decisions. When you're still in the early stages of grief, decision-making should be kept to a minimum. Your judgement and your ability to focus can be clouded for awhile. The only car accident I've had in over 30 years happened about five months after Peter's death. His sister, who had lost not only Peter but also her other brother in the previous seven months, had come out for a visit and we'd been having some very tearful chats. I was taking her with me to the swimming pool for "aquasize" classes. At a T-intersection where I needed to make a left turn, there was a stop sign on the centre median, and while I was watching a car to my right to see if it was slowing down, I was creeping forward, and crashed right into the stop sign. It damaged the under body of my brand new car so

Practical Tips for Living Alone

- When you sit down to eat a meal, always have something living on your table – a fresh flower, fishbowl, candle, plant, etc.
- When you cook a large meal for guests, make extra so you have leftovers, and freeze your own TV dinners.
- Ensure you have a phone beside your bed, with pen and notepaper.
- Adopt a pet!
- Get to know your neighbours by offering to keep an eye on their home when they go away, and they'll do the same for you.
- Keep emergency phone numbers handy and put your next of kin and next door neighbour's numbers on the speed dial.

badly that it had to be towed for repairs. I'm not recommending that grieving people shouldn't drive cars; but I do know that I was not fully concentrating or focussing all my attention at that moment because I was engulfed in grief.

Just living alone is a challenge. It can be lonely. When a household task needs to be done, it's up to you to do it or to pay someone else to do it for you. Cooking meals for one is so challenging, many widows/widowers live on frozen TV dinners. There's no one else to check up on whether you've locked the front door before you went to bed. I learned a lot quickly.

Usually when I have a dilemma, I try to think what Peter would have done. If it's a question about spending money on a gift for someone else, or

Safety Tips for Living Alone

- Make a checklist for locking doors and windows because there's only one person to do it and no one to remind you at night or when you leave the house for a trip or overnight visit.
- Always lock the door at night, or if living in an "unsafe" community, lock it all the time.
- Make sure that your door is solid wood, with no windows nearby. Use a deadbolt lock.
- Install a security system.
- Use the "buddy" system; ask a friend or good neighbour to check on you every 2 or 3 days and do the same for them.
- Don't answer the door after dark unless you are expecting someone by prior arrangement.
- If there isn't a "Neighbourhood Watch" program in your immediate neighbourhood, take positive action and get one started.

buying something beautiful, or paying to do something fun, I know he'd be in favour of it. He was generous to a fault and loved to have a good time. Throughout our entire marriage, I kept track of the money and tried to save it; he loved to spend it. Since his death, I've tried to emulate his generous spirit and have loosened the purse strings considerably. What do I do for other decisions or advice? I call my son or daughter, who inherited so many of his mechanical and artistic talents. And when I can't think what Peter would do or how he might answer troubling questions I write him a letter. This letter is typical:

> …I wish you were here to talk things over with me. I am having such doubts about my faith in God since you left me. I don't really know where you are. Is heaven real? Or are you just ashes that will rise again into the Kingdom of God when Christ returns? Or will He ever return? Is life everlasting or just the memories I have of you that live on? I don't know anything anymore. Whenever I didn't understand something, you were always there to explain. I know I often complained that you explained things in too much technical detail, but I'd give anything right now to listen to one of your explanations or shaggy dog stories which I've heard a hundred times. (Journal, November 2, 2005)

Lack of Appetite

And finally, there is lack of appetite and the need for good nutrition. I often had to remind myself to eat or drink. I simply forgot. For me, this was actually very good news. I had struggled with being overweight most of my life. Now for the first time, the weight fell off without even trying. I was so wrapped up in my grief that the simple pleasure of eating was no longer important to me. My diet changed considerably after Peter's death, because he was a diabetic and needed six small meals a day, high in protein and low in carbohydrates. Of course I had joined him for the same meals. After his death, I cooked fewer meals, ate more fruit, breads and vegetables, and less protein and fat. In the first six months after Peter died, I lost 30 pounds and went from a size 16 to 12. I do not, however, recommend this as a standard weight loss strategy!

Steps to Survival – Stage 3

- ❖ Talk about the death of your loved one. His friends want to know how and why he died, but may be afraid to ask you. Telling the story is a good way to grieve.
- ❖ Take time to make decisions about where you're going to live. Don't rush major decisions.
- ❖ Plan ahead for birthdays, anniversaries and other special dates. Decide what you will do in advance.
- ❖ There is nothing wrong with talking to the dead, nor is there any need to explain. You know what you've experienced.
- ❖ Be receptive to the presence of your loved one. It may be comforting.
- ❖ Take your time going to special places or rooms that scare you. The courage required to go there will come when you're ready to deal with it.
- ❖ Ask a friend or family member to help you go through your loved one's personal belongings.
- ❖ Start sorting with three boxes or bags labelled "garbage" "give away/sell" and "keep".
- ❖ Make a patchwork quilt from your loved one's clothing to keep. It may bring comfort to you or other family members.
- ❖ Relax. Anger and relaxation are incompatible. If we experience one, we can't be experiencing the other at the same time.
- ❖ Meditate, or soak in a hot tub.
- ❖ Laughter is good medicine. Find what you can to make you laugh. Laughing is the best medicine.
- ❖ The power of positive thinking helps you get through almost any challenge. You will feel victorious when you accomplish something difficult.

4

Reflections

By three methods we may learn wisdom: First by reflection, which is noblest; second, by imitation, which is easiest; and third, by experience, which is the bitterest.
(Confucius)

In the weeks after Peter's Celebration of Life service, after family and friends had returned home and some of my new living arrangements were being finalized, I was gradually left with more and more time to think, reflect and ask questions. Though perhaps not aware of it at the time, I was entering Stage 4 of the Grief Process. The stages of grief are often explained in sequence, but the reality of grief is that the emotions of each stage often overlap. For me, reflection overlapped with the pain, lingering guilt and anger more common in Stages Two and Three.

> **Stage 4 of Grief - Depression, Reflection, Loneliness:** Just when your friends may think you should be getting on with your life, a long period of sad reflection will likely overtake you. This is a normal stage of grief, so do not be "talked out of it" by well-meaning outsiders. Encouragement from others is not helpful to you during this stage of grieving. During this time, you finally realize the true magnitude of your loss, and it depresses you. You may isolate yourself on purpose, reflect on things you did with your lost one, and focus on memories of the past. You may sense feelings of emptiness or despair.

About a month after Peter's death, I did feel lonely and depressed, and at various times I felt empty and despairing. For me, Stage Four was primarily one of reflecting and asking questions; such as, where am I going to live? What will I do with the aging Toyota Supra that was Peter's pride and joy, but which had maintenance problems way beyond my ability to handle? What am I going to do about *Wanderlust V,* still tied up at a marina down in Mazatlan, Mexico? The questions about Peter's death were also still there - why did he die? What was the medical reason? Answers to some of these questions became clear within the first few months; others took much longer to be settled.

In the meantime, I was living from day to day, with no dreams for the future, only reflections on what I *didn't* have. All my life I'd always had plans. As soon as one dream was achieved, a new one would emerge. I can still remember them clearly:

1. Graduate from high school
2. Complete university and obtain teaching certificate
3. Marry Peter and have a successful teaching career
4. Travel
5. Raise children
6. Learn to sail
7. Buy a sailboat
8. Build a bigger sailboat
9. Live aboard
10. Sail offshore

What was next? Living alone in a basement suite below my family? Eat, sleep, and what else? Without a goal or a dream, I felt lost and had no reason to get up every morning. I was alone for the very first time in my life, and most of my best friends were offshore cruising. It came as a great shock to me to suddenly realize that there was no one person in this world who loved me above anyone else. I'd never even thought about this before. But it was true. Yes, I knew my children loved me, but they also loved each other. It's only right that my daughter's love for her husband is equal to or even greater than her love for me.

This realization came to me the first time I was physically ill. Peter had always been there for me, especially in the middle of the night. He'd bring me a mug of his special hot toddy, an aspirin, and cold cloths on my forehead to relieve a fever, or he'd massage my legs when I got a muscle cramp. Now I had to ask or tell someone else if I was sick and needed help. I made sure I had a phone beside my bed and the speed dial programmed for my daughter. This helped but it didn't really alter the fundamental reality of my new life.

Choosing Where to Live

The first practical answer to where I should live was answered quickly. It was almost as if God had planned it. Four years earlier, Peter and I had bought a large home in Surrey, British Columbia, in partnership with Tara and her husband Brian. It had a large, lovely two-bedroom in-law suite downstairs and when we bought the house, we had a lawyer help us prepare a written document describing which part of the house belonged to whom and who paid for what costs. The entire lower level of the house, which was roughly one-third of the total floor area of the house, legally belonged to me.

Peter and I had lived in Sidney and Victoria on Vancouver Island for the five years prior to going offshore, and that was where we thought we'd eventually settle. We had dreams of a small waterfront cottage on one of the adjacent Gulf Islands, where we could have *Wanderlust V* moored within sight of our living room window. It would be a place to welcome fellow cruisers to share a meal and stories and to offer cruisers the one thing they all appreciate most – a hot shower! I still would love to live on Vancouver Island or on one of the Gulf Islands; not only because it's a beautiful, laid-back part of the west coast, but because most of my cruising friends who have retired from cruising now live there.

However, once Peter was gone, I knew I needed to be near my family, at least for a while. Tara and Brian had a home and jobs in Vancouver so our house in Surrey provided a centre for the family; for the same reason, this is where Ryan and his family would return. So the basement suite in Surrey was where I would live, at least for the first year, until I knew better where I wanted to go or what I wanted to do with my life.

The current tenants were moving out at the end of May, and a friend of Tara's had spoken for the suite, starting July 1. On May 24th, the day Peter passed away, the new tenant had already written her letter of notice to her current landlord, but for some unknown reason (again, God's plan) she had realized she didn't have to deliver it until May 30th, so she had left it on her kitchen counter. Later that day she got the call to say that Peter was critically ill in Surrey Memorial Hospital. Within days she knew that everything had changed. She tore up the letter and stayed where she was until she could find something else.

My furniture and household items were already in the house, in the unfinished room adjacent to the basement suite. Tara helped me freshen it up with new paint and new colours, and to pick out a few essential new furniture items I needed. About a month after Peter's death, I moved from Tara's guest room into the suite downstairs. Opening and unpacking the boxes that had been in storage for 11 years was somewhat like Christmas. I'd forgotten what lovely things Peter and I had had in our lives before we moved aboard *Wanderlust V* - my favourite teak desk and other teak furniture we'd disassembled to store, the fine art and good books we had collected over the years and the good china and silver I'd kept. It gave me a lot of joy to have them around me again. They made me feel closer to Peter because these were things we had purchased and enjoyed together. Both Tara and Ryan helped me to get settled; hanging pictures, setting up the teak wall unit, and moving furniture around to suit me. Getting settled in to a new home, especially my first "land" home in 11 years, was busy work, just like organizing the funeral had been.

However, always in the back of my mind was the harder question: what about my liveaboard home still moored in Mexico? I missed *Wanderlust V* dreadfully, and worried about whether the caretaker we'd hired was doing a good job of maintaining her. Should I attempt to sell her in Mexico? Or bring her back to Canada? How would I do that? These questions were just too hard. As

Scarlett O'Hara said in *Gone with the Wind*, *"I can't think about that right now. If I do, I'll go crazy. I'll think about that tomorrow."*

Transportation Decisions

Although deciding about what to do with Peter's favourite car, a white Toyota Supra with (removable) Targa Top, was emotionally difficult, it was otherwise fairly easy to settle. I simply couldn't maintain the car myself and I needed transportation. So Tara helped me shop for a new car, both online and by visiting car lots and taking test drives. At first I thought I'd get one that was two or three years old, but when I discovered that a new car would come with a five-year warranty, that really appealed to me.

I found a new car I liked, a Saturn Ion, and for the first time in my life, I had a car that fitted *me*. Peter had stood 6'2" and I was 5' tall; every car we'd ever bought was a compromise. Either I couldn't see over the steering wheel or he didn't have room for his long legs. However, the Saturn fit me perfectly, especially because it was my favourite colour, blue. It was a quad coupe, which suited me perfectly. Most of the time I'd be driving it alone, but if I had grandchildren, the back doors couldn't be opened from inside because they opened in the opposite direction from the front doors. The ads showed a young lady standing between the doors, as if they were hugging her. I called my car "Huggles".

Before I picked up my new car, I spent over an hour just driving around the streets of Richmond in the old Toyota, checking out the house, townhouse and condo where Peter and I had lived over a period of nine years. It was a trip down memory lane, appropriate for my last drive in that sporty white Toyota.

I'm still driving Huggles today and I love it. It did have some major problems during the warranty period, but the work was done free of charge with a loaner provided. Since the warranty expired, there have been no problems. Buying Huggles was a good choice.

The decision to just go out and buy a car was further facilitated by the fact that I was also blessed with financial security. Not only was I eligible to receive 50 percent of both Peter's military and public service pensions on top of my own, he had a supplementary death benefit from the public service equal to two year's salary that was immediately available to me, tax free. Our line of credit at the bank and our Visa card were both life insured and were paid off with little paperwork or trouble.

We had both made wills and given each other power of attorney. So all the legal and financial arrangements were also quite simple. Peter used to joke that I'd be a rich woman without him; in a purely financial sense, he was absolutely right. I have financial security - which means I can afford to live as well as I did before Peter's death. I am grateful that we thought ahead. It made some of these decisions so simple and easy for me.

And I shudder to think how difficult my life might have become, and the uncertainties that might now plague me, if Peter and I had not made the effort, and paid the small expense, to get all our paperwork in order and to make arrangements for either one of us to be financially secure. The peace of mind this brings to the surviving partner is well worth the small investment.

Autopsy Results

My questions about the medical reasons behind Peter's death were all answered when the autopsy was made available about three months after his death. Our family doctor called me and Tara to come in, and we took T'ea with us too. Ryan had already returned to Peru. The doctor told us that there was physical evidence (scar tissue) that indicated a previous heart attack, probably five or ten years ago. Neither Peter nor I were aware of this, but of course many heart attacks are silent ones. Our doctor asked me, "Did Peter ever complain about being tired or suffering indigestion?" I laughed at the irony. Peter could never just sit still and relax. He was always doing something, so he was always tired. He pushed himself hard. And he loved to eat rich, sweet, or fried foods, which of course gave him indigestion. For example, he absolutely loved lemon meringue pie, even though he knew it would give him heart burn. But he'd eat it anyway and then follow it up with a glass of milk to counteract the effects.

The actual cause of his death was cardiac arrhythmia, an irregular beating of the heart, which our doctor said is often sudden and fatal. In Peter's case, he already had a previously damaged heart and his heart had recently undergone major surgery, so when the arrhythmia started, his heart wasn't strong enough to cope.

Learning this additional information actually filled me with deep gratitude for many reasons. Most important, I stopped wondering what had really happened. Now I knew. Secondly, I was so grateful that we'd been home in Canada with our family when his time came; it could just as easily have happened on the boat at sea in the middle of an offshore passage. I shudder at the nightmare of international arrangements that scenario would have produced.

Thirdly, if we had known about his heart condition in 2002 before we left for offshore, I doubt we would have gone. I would have been too afraid that he might have a heart attack at sea. So I realized I should be grateful for the time we'd had. We had enjoyed three years of retirement, being together 24/7 and doing what we enjoyed most – sailing our boat together.

My prayer:
Thank you, God, for giving Peter to me for 41 years of love, joy and adventures.

Grief Therapy

The social worker at the hospital handed me some printed information the day Peter died. It included contact information for a grief therapy group at the Surrey Hospice Society, and, by early fall I started attending sessions there once a week. It really helped me to share feelings, fears and questions with others who were going through similar grief. There were about six of us in the group. Three of us had lost spouses. When you wonder if you're going crazy, it helps to hear from others that they are having the same crazy feelings and thoughts, and you realize that you're not alone. Hearing from a counsellor that all this is a normal part of the grieving process helped too.

Each week there was a sharing/update period, questions for discussion, and sometimes homework. Some of the first questions posed were, "How do I feel? What are my goals? What do I want?" This was my answer: "I feel sad, lonely, lost, in despair, unsure of my future. I hope to get some healing and to feel better physically because aches, anxiety and lack of sleep are all problems."

While attending grief therapy sessions at the Surrey Hospice Society, I had full access to their library and I borrowed many books and took them home to read. Some were written, like this book, by someone who had also gone through grief. My questions about life after death resulted in reading a number of books such as *Life After Life*. The author, Raymond A. Moody, Jr., M.D., investigated more than one hundred independent case studies of people who experienced "clinical death" and were subsequently revived. Their extraordinary stories provided evidence that there is life after physical death. He recounts the testimonies of those who have been to the "other side" and back – all their stories bear striking similarities of an overwhelmingly positive nature. These moving and inspiring accounts helped to give me a glimpse of the peace and unconditional love that awaits us all.

Following the group therapy, I was offered additional counselling as required, and a wonderful volunteer from the society phoned me every week or two just to check up on me. Our chats usually lasted for nearly an hour. She fully understood what I was going through, and she obviously took notes each time, because the next time she called she'd follow up with questions about what I had done, or how her advice had worked for me. I often saved up questions for her too, by writing them down as they occurred. When she realized I was of the Christian faith, she even prayed for me. And when I returned to *Wanderlust V* in Mexico eight months after Peter's death, she gave me her email address so I could write to her about how I was handling that situation. She replied with more comforting words and helpful advice.

Spiritual Questions

After Peter's death, I continued attending Sunday morning services at New Beginnings Community Church with my family. I have always believed there was a God. Peter and I had often paused to gaze in wonder and awe at the sight of his creations – sunsets, stars, flowers, the ocean, etc.. The most awesome of all things created by God is the Sand Dollar. I found several at Bahia Santa Maria on the

Pacific side of the Mexican Baja Peninsula. The largest was more than five inches in diameter. The markings on the shell symbolize the birth, crucifixion and resurrection of Christ. On the top side is an outline of the Easter Lily, at the centre of the Lily is a five-pointed star, representing the Star of Bethlehem. The narrow openings are representative of the nail holes and the spear wound made in the

Sand Dollar

body of Christ during the crucifixion. Reversing the shell you can easily recognize the outline of the Christmas Poinsettia and also the bell. But it was when one of the smaller shells that was wrapped in tissue broke in my luggage, I found three small doves contained inside the shell, no bigger than an eighth of an inch in diameter. The doves represent the Holy Spirit.

In the months after Peter's death I found my own faith deepening and becoming more important to me. Through the Sunday services and messages, women's retreats, ladies Bible studies, other books, Alpha (a non-denominational, six-week program on the basics of Christianity), social gatherings and new friendships, I started to understand what was meant by a personal relationship with Christ, and the need for fellowship within a community of believers. Understanding this was a good start, but I wanted to feel this living faith in my heart and soul. Until I could do that, I still couldn't know for sure whether Peter was in heaven or even if there really is life after death. Or maybe it wasn't that I didn't *know*, I didn't yet *believe!*

Steps to Survival – Stage 4

- ❖ When you start living alone, make sure you have a phone beside your bed and a speed dial for your closest, dearest relative or friend who you can call if you're ill or become suddenly desperate for help in any way.
- ❖ Take your time deciding where you will live and what you will do, but remember family and close friends are important to you at this time. Stay as close to them as possible.
- ❖ Don't be afraid to ask for more details or an autopsy after your loved one's death. It's your right to know.
- ❖ Count your blessings daily; giving thanks that the sun shone today or that a friend called are not trivial matters.
- ❖ Get a list of community resources from the hospital or funeral home and consider attending a grief therapy group. It often helps to share with others who have had a similar loss.
- ❖ If your physical symptoms get so seriously depressing that you're thinking of suicide, seek medical help immediately.
- ❖ If you have questions about your religious faith, spirituality, or visitations, consult your pastor (or other religious leader in your community), social worker or counsellor. Ask for help.
- ❖ Go to the library and search for books on grief recovery. Read!
- ❖ If you're unsure what your talents or spiritual gifts are, ask your pastor or counsellor where and how you can have an evaluation done. The results could change the course of your life.
- ❖ Pray!

5

The Upward Turn

"When one door of happiness closes, another opens; but often we look so long at the closed door that we do not see the one which has been opened for us."

(Helen Keller)

Within a couple of months of Peter's death, I was already settling into my new home in the basement suite, downstairs from Tara and family, and my life was becoming calmer and more organized. Although from time to time I felt pain and depression and still had many questions, a sequence of good events was starting to happen. I believe this was because I was actively searching for answers and for paths to follow. I have always believed that in every cloud there is a silver lining; that for every shattered dream there is a positive new beginning; and that when one door closes, another opens. Every day I was searching for that silver lining, the new beginning and the right door to my future. But I also know that sometimes we have to knock on the door in order for it to open. Often this step can take great courage and strength. I was entering into Stage 5..

> **Stage 5 of Grief – The Upward Turn:** As you start to adjust to life without your dear one, your life becomes a little calmer and more organized. Your physical symptoms lessen, and your "depression" begins to lift slightly

Return to Bluewater Cruising Association (BCA)

After a great deal of thought, I knocked on my first door, about three months after Peter's death. I missed *Wanderlust V* and the cruising life. Many of my best cruising friends were offshore and I was feeling a wave of loneliness It occurred to me that one way to stay connected would be to become actively involved again in the executive of BCA, known as the "Watch". Peter and I had always had the philosophy that the more you give to an organization, the more you get out of it – whether it was a scouting group, a choir, an alumni association or a sailing club.

I called the current Commodore of BCA, who I knew and respected. He also was very aware of my previous involvement with BCA. When I asked him what I could do for the association, he offered me three different opportunities. The one that appealed to me immediately was creating a new position as Archivist. With the Association entering into its 27th year, he and the other executive members felt there was a need to maintain historical records and communicate to current members some of the principles and traditions upon which the association had been founded. I had been a member of BCA for over 20 years, and although I wasn't a founding member myself, I knew all the founding members personally. As editor of *Currents*, BCA's monthly magazine, I had written articles about the founding of BCA, its early beginnings and interviewed and profiled many of those original members. Peter and I had both believed strongly in BCA remaining true to its roots or founding principles.

As official Archivist I started attending regular monthly meetings of the BCA Watch in the fall of 2005, which put me in touch with the current watchkeepers, many of whom I had worked with before. Monthly club nights gave me the opportunity to renew acquaintances with the general membership I already knew and to meet new members. At Watch meetings, I quickly discovered that I could contribute to discussions and general decision-making because my long-standing experience with the Association had taught me as much about the operational side of the organization as I knew about its history. I also started writing a regular archives column in *Currents* every month by researching the records, contacting other members by phone or email, and sometimes actually visiting the Victoria or Calgary chapters to glean more information. I now had a part-time volunteer job, and it felt good to be serving an association I believed in.

Ryan and Family Move to Canada

I had said a tearful goodbye to Ryan, wearing his Dad's Tilley hat, and one-year-old grandson Daryan when they flew back to Peru in June 2005, three weeks after the funeral. Jackie had left the previous day on a different flight via Toronto to have a quick visit with a friend there who had taught with her in Peru. Ryan and I chatted in general about the possibility of me coming to visit the family in Peru, but I didn't really know when I'd see him again. Then, one night in early August, Tara was chatting with him online when she suddenly announced that…

> Ryan has been offered a job in Vancouver, starting August 29th! And plans and paperwork are already well underway for Jackie and the kids to come shortly afterwards. She has an interview for a one-year multiple-entry visa, which was possible because his employer had faxed a letter verifying his one-year contract.
>
> This is *so* exciting. Tara immediately started looking online for rental suites in our area. She and I discussed finding them a small, cheap apartment and paying the first month's rent. It will have to be near public transit so Ryan can get to work. We'll furnish it with used furniture, etc. until they can get on their feet. And, the most wonderful thought of all—I will have all four of my grandchildren here for Christmas this year - what a joy and blessing that will be. (Journal, August 7, 2005)

The job offer came about because Ryan had kept in email contact with friends he had worked with at a delivery firm in Vancouver. The company was aware of his situation – he had a family in Peru so he had been working six months in Canada then returning to Peru for six months. This way he could earn enough money in Canada to support his family in Peru and still do volunteer work there. However, his friend wrote to him telling him the job was his only *if* he would commit to a one-year contract.

I also believe that it was because of Peter's death that Ryan felt a need to return to me and his sister. After all, he was now the man of the family. Nothing could have made me happier! Within a year, Jackie became a permanent resident of Canada and 18 months after their return, their third child was born, a beautiful little girl they named Trea. So then I had five grandchildren, all living close by. Thank you, God!

Learning to Swim

In mid-July, I went to Victoria to visit my lawyer to rewrite my will and to visit friends. While I was there, I met one of their friends, who was also visiting from Surrey. Empathizing with my grief, she invited me to join her "aquasize" classes at a swimming pool in Surrey, near where I lived. She suggested not only would it be good exercise for me, but I would get to meet other women about my age who were also retired. I put it off again and again, but because she was persistent and kept calling, I finally gave in. However, I warned her that I was not really comfortable in the water and that I basically considered myself a non-swimmer. She said that was no problem, we would be exercising in water that would be no higher than my chest. I started attending two to three times a week and I discovered that I really enjoyed it. However, I still could not take my feet off the bottom and actually *swim*.

Just before Christmas, we had Christmas carols playing over the loudspeakers system in the pool. I was singing along as I exercised; then I suddenly noticed what I was doing. I felt *so* good. I lifted my eyes to the warm sunlight shining through the skylights above me and enjoyed the sensation of the warm sun on my face. I smiled with real happiness, perhaps for the first time since Peter's death (other than when baby Daryan arrived as a surprise!). This was a truly a "happy moment".

The term "happy moment" has special significance for me. When Peter and I left to sail offshore, my colleagues had presented me with a special retirement gift, a beautiful leather-bound journal, with a brass cover plate engraved, "A Sailor's Write Book". I had decided I would use it exclusively to record happy moments while we were offshore. Usually these were moments of pure joy that brought tears to my eyes.

Now, when I felt this happy moment in the swimming pool before Christmas, I also experienced pangs of guilt. How could I be happy when I had lost the person I loved most in the world? I should be miserable and mourning. But I *was* happy. And many more happy moments were to come.

Later, my new "aquasize" instructor offered to give me swimming lessons for 15 or 20 minutes after the class was over, before the pool became filled with other activities. I was reluctant about that too. I had taken swimming lessons as a kid and failed the Red Cross Beginner's test because I couldn't float on my back or tread water. I'd taken lessons again when I was in university and not only did I fail once more, but the overworked and incompetent instructor had told me I was a "sinker" and had given up on me. This totally discouraged me from ever trying again. Peter was the only one who knew this story and understood my sensitivity and embarrassment. Although he was an excellent swimmer and diver himself, and enjoyed it immensely, he never pushed me about it or told others that I couldn't swim. However, on the boat we made sure there were jack lines (to which to tether) and inflatable PFDs (personal floatation devices like a life jacket) and that we were both attached to something fixed and rigid when we were at sea or in any rough conditions. I had sailed 29,000 miles safely, without ever having to swim, secure in my belief that it was more important to stay *on* the boat, than being able to swim back *to* it. I still believe that - in theory - but I've now discovered that swimming is also an enjoyable and wonderful skill for any sailor to have.

My new swimming instructor spent considerable time with me at the shallow end of the wave pool; slowly and patiently she had me floating on my back – a miracle! After that we got into treading water and practising various swimming strokes. I was on my way – I could swim!

Wanderlust V Comes Home

I've already described the challenge of returning to *Wanderlust V* and sailing her across the Sea of Cortes to La Paz. Once I had loaded her on the Dockwise ship in Mexico, I flew home to Canada to meet her. That was an exciting, happy time for me and my family. Ryan and Tara helped me offload *Wanderlust V* in Nanaimo and sail her to her new home, Captain's Cove Marina in Ladner, about a 30-minute drive from where I lived in Surrey. En route, under full sail and blue skies – the perfect moment – we scattered Peter's ashes in the Strait of Georgia, from the side deck of the boat he'd built and loved – just as he would have wanted. We each took a turn, one after each other, scattering a portion of the ashes and quietly praying and bidding him farewell. When we arrived at the marina, good friends and family were waiting with a bouquet of flowers and big smiles, to greet us and take our lines. *Wanderlust V* was "home". We celebrated!

Wanderlust V is Home, September 2005

That summer *Wanderlust V* was away from the dock on many occasions. I was always accompanied by other family members as crew and sometimes one or two of their friends. We sailed in the Gulf Islands, along the inside coastline of Vancouver Island, the Howe Sound area north of Vancouver, and back and forth across the Georgia Strait. The highlight for me was sailing into Montague Harbour in August 2006 for the BCA Farewell to the Fleet Rendezvous – the same annual rendezvous that had wished Peter and I *bon voyage* when we had left to sail south to Mexico in August 2002. It was an incredibly happy moment for me, complete with tears of joy. Later, several BCA friends who had seen me bring her into the harbour that day told me they also had tears in their eyes. How wonderful it felt that there were others who had missed *Wanderlust V* and were joyous that she had returned!

We had many other adventures that summer – some joyous and others challenging. We caught crab in Ganges Harbour and enjoyed many crab feasts in the cockpit. The hydraulic steering broke in Howe Sound and we were towed to False Creek for repairs. We explored new destinations such as Granite Falls, at the end of Indian Arm, and took a friend out sailing serenely in English Bay, while we devoured lemon meringue pie from the Granville Island Market. We returned to favourite anchorages like Plumper's Cove, Halkett Bay and Clam Bay. We visited friends on Saltspring Island and had an unofficial BCA rendezvous at their home with other cruising friends. Such joy! And such a sense of self-satisfaction that the family Peter had left behind could actually do all this! At the end of the summer, I calculated I had sailed *Wanderlust V* another 1,000 nautical miles since Peter's death.

Old and New Friends

Friends were extremely important to me after Peter's death and provided much support. We had had hundreds of acquaintances, especially his military colleagues who'd been neighbours or with whom he'd worked over his 25-year career. After he retired, we met hundreds of cruisers through BCA, at marinas where we had lived, or on our offshore voyages. Starting in 1967, we had sent out a Christmas newsletter, called "The Doherty Journal " every year and although the list was smaller at first when it involved typing, running off copies on a Gestetner, and putting them in stamped envelopes, it grew to over 200 in the late 1990s once we were on the internet with email. Sometimes I'd say to Peter, "We haven't heard from so-and-so for three years now; I think we should drop them from the list." but Peter would insist, "Let's just send one more and add a personal note that we're sorry we haven't heard from them in a long time!" And he would do so, year after year, until the letter or email came back "address unknown". I learned a lot about friendship from Peter. He was *my* best friend forever but he worked hard to maintain friendships with everyone he met.

Having this list of friends was a blessing when Peter passed away because I could send out one email to all our friends letting them know of his passing. I quickly heard from many of them, but gradually our contacts lessened, even though each Christmas I still sent them a newsletter.

However, there was a group of three other couples Peter and I had met while stationed in Zweibrücken, Germany, and we have all remained best friends to this day - Ken and Penny Carpenter, Jean and Harley Ranson and Ray and Bobann Dziver. They still phone, email me and welcome me and my family for dinner or as overnight guests in their homes, which are spread across Canada from Sidney, British Columbia, to Toronto, Ontario. The Carpenters and Ransons lived on the same street as Peter and I in Germany, and throughout the years we've often lived on the same street again. When we arrived in Ottawa in 1970, all three couples were there and the Ransons were on the same street as we were. Shortly after we arrived in Greenwood, Nova Scotia, in 1981, the Carpenters arrived and moved in on the same street. After Peter died, Penny came over immediately from Sidney to be at my side and her husband Ken spoke at Peter's Celebration of Life service. I often stop at the Dziver's home in Kelowna en route to visit Calgary relatives, and I've had two trips east where I've stayed overnight with Ransons and attended theatre productions at Stratford and Niagara-on-the Lake with them. None of these friends became sailors like we did, but they've all been aboard *Wanderlust V* at one point or another and cheered us on our voyages. They've all also continued supporting me throughout my voyage to the other side of grief.

Likewise, there are cruising friends, like Barb Angel and Ian Monsarrat, who we met back in the early 1990s; we subsequently became neighbours in the same marina. Barb is a fiery redhead with a Newfie accent. She's as honest as the day is long and both she and Ian are hard workers who have hearts of gold, always ready to help. They've cruised offshore and lived aboard their boat for over 30 years. They were our best friends, the last friends to visit Peter before he came home from the hospital. Since his death, they have been beside me on numerous occasions—handling the guest book and CDs at Peter's service, taking me sailing with them on their boat, spending time together at my home, or restaurant dinners prior to BCA club nights or other meetings. But the most wonderful thing they did was to come with me to Mexico after Peter's death. They provided a shoulder to cry on and physical labour to pull *Wanderlust V* back together after she had been sitting at a dock for eight months.

We met Jackie and Manfred Melzer through BCA just before we left on our first offshore cruise in 1989 and they were there to welcome us when we came home in 1990. They have been good friends ever since. Jackie and I worked together on a BCA 20th anniversary cookbook and Peter and Manfred traded tips about boat building, as they also built their own boat. In the late fall of 2004, they came down to boat-sit *Wanderlust V* in Mexico for three months while we returned home for medical visits, Christmas with the family, and later while we returned yet again to Canada to attend Peter's brother's funeral. Once *Wanderlust V* was back in Canada, they helped me unload boat parts and deliver them to a boater's consignment store.

Last but not least, there is Sally Holland, also a BCA member, who was the only widow friend I had when Peter died. Over the years she sailed with us aboard *Wanderlust V* and often invited us to her lovely floating home, not only for dinners but for overnight accommodation when we were living in Sidney. She was there to meet *Wanderlust V* at the dock in when we arrived back in Canada in 2006. When Peter died, she gave me lots of suggestions and support, some of which I've included in this book. She also helped proofread this book.

As I have written before, friends were always important to both Peter and myself. However, since his death I have come to understand how truly blessed we are when we have good, dependable friends. Not everyone we think of as friends will prove to be there when we need them. Are we always there for our friends? We may not even know who our true friends are until tragedy or real difficulties hit us. Even good friends can find it hard to know how best to help us during the different phases of our voyage of grief. Sometimes we must make the effort to reach out to them and give them opportunities to support us. Asking for help can be hard, but I've found that friends *want* to be asked.

Not only have I been blessed to have long-time friends still supporting me but, in the years after Peter's death, I have made many new acquaintances through attending New Beginnings Community Church and through singing with the Maple Leaf Singers, a non-profit 60+ voice fabulous show chorus that entertain all over the lower mainland of British Columbia and have a lot of fun doing it. Many of these folks, who Peter never even met, are now becoming my close friends. One in particular is Netty Lopez. She arrived in Surrey from California to live downstairs from her son and his family after she retired, which was about the same time as I moved into the suite below my daughter's family after Peter's death. We lived within walking distance of each other, we were both single seniors in a young vibrant church and soon found we had many interests in common. We have become close friends who chat on the phone regularly, trade books, travel and go out for lunches, movies and theatre together. We also share the job of coordinating the Greeting Ministry at New Beginnings Community Church, and she dog sits for me whenever I'm away travelling. We were even baptised on the same day by Netty's son, Pastor Ian Lopez. I regularly thank God for bringing Netty into my life, and realize that if Peter were still alive, I'd never have known this friendship.

Crewing Offshore

Another wonderful thing that happened the summer that *Wanderlust V* returned was that my very good BCA friends, Peter McMartin and Connie Monahan, who were currently cruising their boat in the South Pacific, invited me to join them as crew in New Caledonia aboard their Peterson 36 cutter, *SV Cookie Cutter*, to make the 700-mile passage with them from New Caledonia to Australia. I knew they were excellent sailors and that their boat was well-built, strong and seaworthy. So I flew to Noumea in October of 2006, and spent three weeks just cruising and exploring the tropical waters of New Caledonia. I absolutely loved it! One of the highlights was that

I had brought snorkel gear with me, even though I had never snorkelled in my life. Connie spent a few minutes with me on a beach showing me the basics, being very helpful and patient. My first float over a bommie (a shallow isolated piece of reef located a short distance offshore) seeing a small fish and sponges through my goggles was pure magic for me

I had several more occasions to snorkel after that, but the highlight came the day we sailed into Mato Islet, in the lagoon south of the Grand Isle of New Caledonia. We anchored in 25 feet of water over a sand bottom and snorkelled the reef in the lee of the island. Up until that time, I had only swum in a swimming pool, so for the first time ever, I summoned up all my courage and slid into 25 feet of water off the side of the inflatable dinghy. I spent about 15 minutes floating over and around the reef, looking at the most beautiful coral - purple, pink, green and yellow - plus many colourful tropical fish. I never knew coral was coloured. All I'd ever seen was dead coral, which is white. At one point, I was over a canyon 30 feet deep.

SV Cookie Cutter, New Caledonia, 2006

That was scary – but I was doing it! Seeing this absolutely incredibly beautiful sight under water was a tremendous thrill - and I could never have done it if I hadn't learned how to swim.

During the four weeks I spent on the sailboat with my friends, I learned a lot about myself. Their boat was very different from *Wanderlust V*. I had never before used self-tailing winches; it scared me not to hold onto the sheet or to cleat it off. Their autopilot worked very differently from the Wagner that we had on *Wanderlust V*, so I had difficulty knowing when to correct it. When we made the 700-mile passage to Australia, their boat was not nearly as steady in heavy winds and seas because it didn't have a full keel like *Wanderlust V* did. Even on a reach or close hauled, there was a lot of side-to-side movement. At one point in the voyage as we approached the Australian coast in the dark, we were reluctant to enter a shallow bay at the estuary, as we had a 25-knot following wind, so we "heaved to" – which means we stopped the boat's forward motion by balancing rudder against the sail. This was another new experience for me. Never in all the ocean miles I'd sailed on *Wanderlust V* had this ever been necessary, but on *Cookie Cutter*, it gave us much needed relief so we could take turns getting a good sleep. The motion had made me a bit queasy and certainly dampened my appetite, but I enjoyed announcing when I got home that "On the *Cookie Cutter*, I did *not* lose my cookies."

Despite the joy of learning about a new country, snorkelling coral reefs, handling a different boat, and cooking aboard, I missed Peter terribly. One day I was sitting on the beach while my friends were off exploring, and I thought how hard it was to be there without him. I cried for him. What was I doing? Experiencing all these adventures and beauty without him? It just wasn't as much fun as I thought it would be.

On the boat, I volunteered to do a fair bit of the cooking and wash-up in the galley, because that's something I love to do; and I realized how much I missed it at home, living downstairs from Brian and Tara. Although I usually made my own coffee, simple breakfast and light lunch, I regularly ate dinner upstairs with the family. I decided that when I returned home, I would institute a new tradition – "Sunday dinner at Grandma's". That meant that Brian, Tara, Te'a and Matthew would be invited to make the big trip down the stairs once a week to Grandma's house to join me for dinner at my dining room table, eat off my good china, and enjoy (hopefully!) different foods than they normally cooked in their own busy household. I had many recipes that had been family favourites when my kids had been growing up.

Adopting a Puppy

I returned home to British Columbia to some very happy events; the first of which was to adopt a nine-week old black and white female Havanese puppy who I named "Tilley". I'd been without a dog for over three years, which is the longest ever, since receiving my first dog when I was only six. Now that I was living alone, I knew that a dog would be wonderful company. I wanted a small dog that could sit on my lap, but I didn't want a yappy one! So Tara and I researched breeds, toured pet stores, checked out breeders on the internet, and discovered that the Havanese breed was exactly what I was looking for: small, non-shedding, smart, affectionate, playful and most important, non-verbal. Tilley is all that, and *very* much loved and spoiled.

Tilley 2011

The last dog Peter and I had had was a mixed breed, mostly Sheltie, named Ship's Dog Princess. She lived to be 17. She sailed with us on both our offshore trips in 1989 and 2002 and lived aboard continuously for the last nine years of her life. Her ashes are scattered in the Sea of Cortes. For anyone grieving the death of a beloved pet dog, I'd like to share with you how I picture Princess with Peter today.

Just this side of heaven is a place called Rainbow Bridge.
When an animal dies that has been especially close to
someone here,
that pet goes to Rainbow Bridge.
There are meadows and hills for all of our special friends so
they can run and play together.
There is plenty of food, water and sunshine, and our
friends are warm and comfortable.
All the animals who had been ill and old are restored to
health and vigour.
Those who were hurt or maimed are made whole and
strong again,
just as we remember them in our dreams of days and times
gone by.
The animals are happy and content, except for one small
thing;
they each miss someone very special to them, who had to
be left behind.
They all run and play together, but the day comes when
one suddenly stops and looks into the distance.
His bright eyes are intent. His eager body quivers.
Suddenly he begins to run from the group, flying over the
green grass,
his legs carrying him faster and faster.
You have been spotted, and when you and your special
friend finally meet,
you cling together in joyous reunion, never to be parted
again.
The happy kisses rain upon your face; your hands again
caress the beloved head,
and you look once more into the trusting eyes of your pet,
so long gone from your life but never absent from your
heart.
Then you cross Rainbow Bridge together....

(Author unknown)

Gratitude

It was about this time I started giving praise and thanks to God in a very big way. Every night it became a ritual for me before I fell asleep to thank God for giving me another day and for all my blessings; I would list them all off — my children, grandchildren, friends, home, puppy, *Wanderlust V*, and anything special or good that had happened that day and, finally, for giving Peter to me for 41 wonderful years. My only request, which came at the end, was always the same: "And please...give me guidance, courage and strength to make it through tomorrow."

A Temporary Downward Turn and Counselling

It was a good thing that I'd had this surge of gratitude for all my blessings, because the upward turn started to *swing downward* in a big hurry...

In the winter of 2007, when we decided as a family the time had come to sell *Wanderlust V*, we proceeded to strip her of 11 years worth of personal effects and clutter in order to make her as attractive as possible to potential buyers. Her waterline rose several inches as a result. On the Easter weekend, Ryan and I decided to take her out sailing for the day with three-year-old Daryan and Tilley, both in life jackets. Just as we were entering the north arm of the Fraser River, all the engine instruments went to zero, despite the fact the engine was running. Rushing down below to investigate, I saw smoke. "Fire!" I shouted. I headed up onto deck as Ryan came down below and immediately started squelching flames in the engine room with a fire extinguisher. When he saw more smoke coming from behind the panel above the chart table, he tore the panel off to cut wires behind it that were burning. I turned the boat around and headed back to the safety of sea, steering manually and taking frequent bearings of our position, knowing we might lose all our electronic instruments. I was shaking with fear like I'd never known. Fortunately, the engine remained running.

We opened all the hatches to clear the smoke and spent six hours nervously motoring back to Ladner, where we tied her up safely at the dock, turned off the engine and switched off everything electrical. We didn't attempt to clean up anything. I knew an insurance adjuster would need to see it all. I heaved a huge sigh of relief, gave a small prayer of thanks for everyone's safety and went home to call the insurance company.

Of course I'd had anxiety before, but the saga of the year-long electrical repairs was the worst anxiety I've ever experienced. Every time the electrician went to repair one thing, another problem would be discovered. The boat had to be hauled out and she spent several months in a boat yard, and so I was paying fees to keep her in the yard *and* paying fees to reserve my slip at the marina – double rent! It was over eight months before she returned to the dock from the yard, where I'd parted with huge sums of money, paying electricians to completely rewire the boat, and in the course of those repairs, discovering and repairing other problems. I received very little from the insurance company, as there was no way to separate the cost of the repairs due to the fire from the cost of the required upgrade to a 20-year-old electrical system. Even back at the dock, I learned there was still some electrical work outstanding. The reason it took so long was because the company I hired was a small, two-man operation, and they were working on as many as six boats at a time, so they were only giving *Wanderlust* V part-time attention.

Managing this complex, expensive electrical repair project was way beyond my capabilities, yet I was the owner and the person footing the bill. I was waking up with my thoughts in turmoil and my stomach in knots, afraid for the future of *Wanderlust V* and me. I couldn't sell the boat in the condition she was in, and in the meantime I was paying huge amounts of money for repairs and rented space. In the end, the boat was in such a mess from being pulled apart to get at wiring behind bulkheads and lockers that I had to hire a detailer to come in to do cosmetic repairs, paint and varnish. 2007 was a bad year.

It was during this time that I realized I was actually going through a second period of grief. The first was after Peter died; this second period was seeing *Wanderlust V* dying and leaving me. The idea of selling her was sad enough, but seeing her interior being ripped apart and the resulting mess was like seeing a close friend being operated on or dying a slow death. She was like a cancer victim with a very uncertain future—would anyone ever love her and sail her again? I was powerless to save her and return to the carefree cruising life Peter and I had enjoyed.

I grieved all over again. My anxiety was so severe I was waking up when was still dark out, with knots in my stomach, and couldn't get back to sleep. Fortunately I knew enough to know I needed professional help. I consulted Irene Flett of Coastal Counseling, recommended by Tara and Pastor Ian. Irene was a Registered Clinical Counsellor with years of experience and a very nice person. I started seeing Irene on a weekly basis over a period of several months. My first appointment was draining. She dug pretty deep, making me verbalize my fears, reliving once again the shock of Peter's death, the pain, guilt, doubts and depression I'd experienced in the last two years and now the severe anxiety I was suffering. Telling my fears to a perfect stranger in the first hour was overwhelming. But I knew it was necessary in order to deal with my debilitating anxiety attacks. Irene was wonderful and just what I needed. She listened, understood, and asked questions to get me to clarify my feelings for myself. She also offered much practical advice and suggested reading materials. On our second appointment...

…we discussed my early morning anxiety and came up with a new routine for me -

- get up when I wake up (which of course would be really early),
- have a cup of tea or hot water with lemon,
- step outdoors and soak up some light (or better still, take Tilley for a walk), and
- thank God for another day and all the beauty in His world and ask Him to guide me.

When I came back home, I would have a shower, get dressed, and eat breakfast. Hopefully by then, the family upstairs would be up and I could join them with my pot of coffee. After a visit there, I would come back downstairs and begin 'work', ticking off items on my to-do list. She told me to remember that I can only do one thing at a time, and that every morning a list of things to do will be waiting. The added advantage of getting up so early is that I may actually be tired enough to go to bed earlier or have an afternoon nap. I must do this every day until my next appointment. (Journal, July 30, 2007)

Aside from this very practical advice, Irene taught me one simple but very effective technique to relieve the knots in my stomach — yoga breathing. When I woke up with these symptoms in the morning, I'd lie on my back, place one hand on my belly, and slowly and deeply breathe in, expanding my stomach (not my chest or lungs) then slowly exhale and feel my stomach flatten. It worked. The knots were gone and it forced my mind to concentrate on something practical, rather than random fears. I continue to use this technique whenever I'm nervous or anxious.

One of the books Irene recommended was *Calm My Anxious Heart* by Linda Dillow. I found this especially good. Linda says that we women worry a lot—about our children, our friends, our careers, our families and our finances. We want to be content and to trust God with our worries, but it's a struggle to let go and free ourselves from the burden of anxiety. Her book is filled with encouragement and practical help for overcoming anxiety, including a 12-week Bible study to help you discover what the Bible says about contentment and ways to apply it in daily life.

After several sessions, when I asked Irene, "Who am I as a person? What am I going to do with my life?" she recommended I do a Spiritual Gifts Evaluation. Three of my friends agreed to fill out the questionnaire independently, and I did one myself. Irene tabulated the results and the top two were pretty much what I expected—Hospitality and Administration. This encouraged me to volunteer to serve as a part-time administrator for New Beginnings Community Church and to think actively about social events I could host for the church or for BCA. The third gift was Leadership, which came as a total surprise. In my career and in my volunteer duties with BCA, I had always seen myself as a detail and support person – an administrator. Peter was the leader or the president or the commodore, and I was the one who followed behind him, reminding him of people's names, keeping track of our finances and social calendar, and providing him with encouragement and support. Knowing I had the gift of leadership gave me encouragement when later I was elected to serve as Commodore for BCA. I was beginning to see several new challenging but enjoyable roles for me in my life.

A Cruise around South America

A year after this grief counselling I enjoyed the cruise of a lifetime. I'd always wanted to go on a cruise ship, which Peter just laughed at, saying "We've got our own ship to cruise." But I just thought how nice it would be to go on a trip and be waited on. We wouldn't have to change the oil, clean the head or scrub the decks. I celebrated my 65th birthday on board *MV Discovery*, with my SIL (sister-in-law), Jennifer, who was celebrating her 60th birthday. It was an eight-week cruise around South America. I enjoyed seeing tango dancers in Argentina, walking with the penguins in Antarctica, exploring the Moai statues on Easter Island, seeing giant turtles in the Galapagos Islands, climbing up over the rise to see Machu Pichu for the first time in Peru, transiting the Panama Canal, buying molas from the San Blas Island natives, and visiting a coffee plantation in beautiful Costa Rica. I'd always hoped that when Peter and I sailed across the South Pacific, I'd see the Galapagos, Easter Island and Robinson Crusoe Island. Even though it was without Peter, I did it - so this was a dream that finally came true for me.

In conclusion, although the first two years after Peter's death gave me lots of exciting opportunities, this period in my life was still a struggle. For example, American friends Peter and I had met in Mexico came to visit. I had a wonderful time taking them over to Vancouver Island and showing them some beautiful scenery, including the Butchart Gardens. They invited me to join them at their timeshare at Whistler. It was a lovely visit, but I couldn't help but reflect how sad it was that Peter was not with me to share it.

I also started taking piano lessons – something I'd always wanted to do but never had the time. But now it made me miss *his* piano playing. I was planning on selling *Wanderlust V*, which can be viewed positively as moving on with my life; but it was still stressful - emotionally, physically and financially. Life was getting better, but sometimes the days were a tough slog.

Steps to Survival – Stage 5

- ❖ Don't be afraid to knock on doors by volunteering to help someone or a cause you believe in.
- ❖ As long as you can handle it, accept as many invitations as you can, to do something new or different, in order to find out what you'd like to do with the rest of your life.
- ❖ When you do have a happy moment, don't feel guilty. You are recovering!
- ❖ A pet can be a wonderful companion if you're living alone.
- ❖ Give thanks every day for your blessings, even if it's only because the sun shone or a friend called.
- ❖ If depression or anxiety get worse, seek a referral to a professional counsellor.
- ❖ Practice yoga breathing to relieve anxiety symptoms.
- ❖ Read books on grief recovery, life after death, or the Bible.
- ❖ Never pass up an opportunity to meet someone new or learn something new.
- ❖ Ask your counsellor to do a Spiritual Gifts Assessment. Your results may surprise you and will teach you more about who you are.
- ❖ Pray for guidance, courage and strength to get through each day.

6

Figuring it Out

Be still and know that I am God.
(Psalm 46:10)

When someone we love dies we may feel extremely confused about many things because that death changes everything – how we live, where we live, who we live with. We may even feel that our whole world has collapsed and we are searching for meaning and purpose in our lives. These feelings are normal. In the numbness after the death, in the months of getting practical living arrangements reorganized, we may be able to push away the deeper uncertainties and keep ourselves busy to avoid facing them. But as the months go by and we continue to move slowly forward through the stages of grief, our deeper questions will call out to be answered. Facing them will take courage. Yet, from my own experience, I've learned that as we work to find answers and resolve them for ourselves, burdens are lifted from our shoulders and acceptance and hope seem closer.

These big questions will be unique to each of us, but I believe that hearing other people's questions and how they found answers can encourage us to seek our own answers. It is in this spirit that I've written this book and I would like to share the three most significant and difficult questions I struggled with after that awful day when Peter died. My questions were: wondering what to do with *Wanderlust V* now that I'd lost her skipper; finding answers to my spiritual questions; and, understanding who I am and how to rebuild my life without the man I loved so much.

It's taken me more than six years of reflection and prayer, and the support of many friends to begin to figure things out; but today answers to my three questions are steadily becoming clearer. I had come to the sixth stage of grief.

Stage 6 of Grief – Reconstruction & Working Through: As you become more functional, your mind starts working again, and you will find yourself seeking realistic solutions to problems posed by life without your loved one. You will start to work on practical and financial problems and reconstructing yourself and your life without him or her.

The Boat Decision

Deciding what to do with *Wanderlust V* was difficult emotionally, financially and physically. Emotionally because, with all the moving around we did, it really was the only home our family knew. Peter and I lived in 22 homes during our 41 years of marriage, and the record for the longest time in one *house* was the four years we lived in California from 1976-80. However, *Wanderlust V* not only sat in many of those back yards, she had been a part of our lives for a total of 25 years and we had lived aboard for 13 of those. As my daughter recently wrote, "In all the ways that matter, she was my home growing up."

To Peter and me, *Wanderlust V* was our third child. We had given birth to her with all the anticipation, love and labour pains (no pun intended) that had accompanied Ryan and Tara's births. We had designed every inch of her interior, sail plan and deck plan. When we took delivery of the hull, I started a meticulous record of expenses, so that we would know how much it cost to build her and how much we had saved by doing the work ourselves. At the end of the first year, the bills for materials, tools and services came to $50,000 and that didn't include the purchase price of the hull which was over $30,000. That's when I stopped keeping track! I didn't want to know.

Peter was chief engineer and designer, but all the family worked long hours to build her together. The hull was delivered to our back yard in Ottawa in 1980, and the kids were called upon at an early age to carry 35 lb. lead ingots up the 12-foot staircase to her deck and slide them down into her empty keel, after Peter and I had finished the hot, dirty work of melting down 11,000 pounds of scrap lead in the garage, skimming the sludge off the top with a soup ladle, and pouring the clean lead into bread loaf pans we used as moulds. Later the operation moved to the interior of the boat, where we melted down the clean ingots, poured the molten lead over and between them, installing keel bolts at the same time.

Eight years and 5,000 highway miles later, it was with tears of joy on my part, a happy grin on my husband's face, and the kids running around trying to help in every way they could, that *Wanderlust V* was launched at Steveston Harbour in Richmond, British Columbia, on Canada's Pacific coast. Although Reliance Sailcraft produced 46 hulls, each one of them was custom finished by their owners, and so there's not another boat like her in the world. We had built her, she was ours, and she was beautiful.

We put nearly 15,000 sea miles under her keel in the first two years, cruising the BC Coast and doing a one-year offshore passage from Vancouver to Mexico, across to Hawaii, north to Alaska and home again. We spent the next 12 years exploring the Gulf and San Juan Islands, sailing almost all the way around Vancouver Island and up the BC Coast as far as the Broughton Archipelago. In 2002, Peter and I both retired from the federal government, and left for offshore again, hopefully to sail around the world very slowly, savouring every port and every new adventure along the way, in our search for endless summer. By the time we got to Mazatlan, Mexico, in 2005, *Wanderlust V* had logged a total of 29,000 miles under her keel since her launching in 1988.

After all the sweat and tears, the miles she had sailed, and the 25 years she had been part of our family, *Wanderlust V* was more than just a boat. She was our home, we loved her with a passion, and the thought that she would not continue to be part of our family was like giving up one of our children for adoption.

But what price do we put on something we love? *Wanderlust V* had been our magic carpet that could take Peter and I anywhere in the world we wanted to go; she introduced us to new friends and new places, she was our home, our life, our future.

However, Peter's sudden death put me and the boat into a new situation. Did I really want to continue to sail her or was I ready to let go of that dream? I actually had lots of options to consider. I could keep her in Mexico as my winter condo. I could keep her in BC and continue to sail the BC coastline. I could sell her in Mexico or sell her in BC. I could sail her back to BC or ship her back. I could head offshore again with crew. However, without Peter, none of those options involving sailing the boat offshore or keeping her in Mexico were particularly attractive. I realized when I was in New Caledonia on board *Cookie Cutter* that I was subconsciously surrendering the dream of sailing her offshore to someone else.

I knew I did not want to sail alone, with part-time crew who did not have the same love and commitment to *Wanderlust V* that Peter and I had had. I'd heard lots of horror stories about the difficulty of keeping good crew. When their cash ran out or they had a family emergency at home or they decided they wanted to sail in a different direction than the owner, they could abandon your boat in any foreign port to fly home or just jump ship. The thought of being left alone on the boat in a foreign port without crew was scary. And without Peter, it just wasn't as much fun.

The option I was left with was to bring *Wanderlust V* back to Canada from Mexico, and to sail her in local waters. I also realized that there was another good reason to bring her back to BC. My family, including my grandchildren, needed to have an opportunity to sail her again. They were already dealing with their own grief at losing their father and grandfather; to sell *Wanderlust V* in Mexico meant they would never see her or sail on her again. T'ea and Matthew had sailed with us for four summers before we left for offshore in 2002. It had been one of our greatest joys as grandparents. Angie and Daryan had never even seen the boat, but had heard so much about her, they knew that she was an important part of their family.

A temporary plan started to emerge. If I could somehow arrange to sail or ship her back home to BC, then we could sail her in BC waters until such time as we could make more concrete decisions about her future. I decided to return to Mazatlan, check out all systems to ensure she was seaworthy, find crew, and sail her to La Paz, which was the port from which she could be shipped home on Dockwise Yacht Transport.

As I previously described in Chapter 5, I sailed *Wanderlust V* across the Sea of Cortes, then had her shipped back to Canada. After she returned to British Columbia in June 2006, my family and I had an incredibly happy summer, sailing the BC coastline and Gulf Islands. At the end of that summer, with such good feelings of self-satisfaction, I knew I wasn't ready to part with her...quite yet. Neither was Ryan. My wise daughter Tara said, "You'll know when the time is right, Mom." I paid for a full year of moorage.

That winter, *Wanderlust V* was tied to the dock while I was off for eight weeks to New Caledonia and Australia, and the kids checked out the boat and maintained her in my absence. When I came back in December, I went down to see her myself and I had tears in my eyes seeing her sitting there looking sad. It seemed so strange that no one was living aboard or sailing her.

I realized how wrong it was for her to sit at the dock. Not only did I not want to sail her offshore without Peter, I realized it was not right to keep her for the purpose of weekend sailing in BC either. We'd only sailed 20 days out of the 365 that year and it was costing me about $1,000 per month for moorage, insurance and maintenance. That's about $600 per sailing day!

How priorities had changed! In the first few years after she was launched, Peter and I and our two teenagers had sailed her in BC waters at every possible opportunity – summer or winter. And when the kids left home, Peter and I moved aboard and we sailed every weekend or holiday. Now, everything was different. My kids had jobs, homes, school, growing families, other friends. I could not handle 51 feet of boat alone. *Wanderlust V* was not doing what she was meant to do.

> *"A ship in a harbour is safe, but that's not what ships are for."*
> (Anon.)

When *Wanderlust V* sailed on a close reach in a stiff breeze, Peter used to say, "She lifted up her skirts and flew." Translation: she heeled to one side so much she showed her pretty bottom! She loved to sail – and sail fast – not sit at a dock. And so I knew the time had come to sell; it wasn't right to keep her tied up. Tara said she was Okay with whatever I wanted to do; but what about Ryan? I bided my time until one day in February 2007, when quite out of the blue, Ryan said, "When are you going to call a broker and list the boat for sale, Mom?" That's the cue I had been waiting for.

I smiled and replied, "Just as soon as you help me clear out all the personal stuff and clean her up for showing!" We all agreed she was meant to be sailed and loved, and that we were doing what was best for her. So we spent several weekends clearing personal items off and sprucing her up.

I've already explained (in Chapter 3) the challenge of the electrical fire following our cleanup and the subsequent repairs that delayed the sale. However, she was sold in June 2009. It was a bittersweet moment for me – relief that my financial responsibilities were over and joy that *Wanderlust V* would sail again. Her new owner, Andy Cain, referred to us as "...the family that first breathed life, soul and spirit into *Wanderlust V* when she was just a bare hull and deck." I was confident our boat would continue to be sailed and loved as we had loved her.

But was selling the boat the best thing for our family? As much as they loved her too, I think as time goes on, both Ryan and Tara realized that keeping her in the long term was a beautiful dream, but an impractical and well nigh impossible one. They were busy with their own children, careers and struggling to make ends meet financially. I could scarcely afford to keep her; they definitely couldn't.

Another consideration was my health. By the time we sold her, I was scheduled to go in for surgery to replace my right hip, which had deteriorated due to osteoarthritis. As soon as I had recovered about 90 per cent of my strength in that hip, I started having trouble with my right knee – more osteoarthritis. Today I know that I do not have the physical mobility nor the quick reflexes required on an offshore sailboat. I can't put all my weight on my right leg, which any sailor will know makes sailing on a port tack very difficult. I'm not saying my days on the water are over; I would probably enjoy cruising on a power boat in local waters with competent crew, or even on a sailboat in light winds and calm seas. But once you're out on the open water, there's never any guarantee it's going to stay that way. You have to be prepared to deal with any emergency or change in weather. I may be prepared mentally; but physically I'm no longer up to it.

Yes, I think we made the right decisions at each stage for all the right reasons. It's just that it's taken me over six years to fully understand how and why these steps fell into place and to accept the loss. Though we had good reasons, it was still *hard* to do. This is the email I sent out to friends and family on July 14, 2009:

> Just wanted to let you know that as of June 30, 2009, *Wanderlust V* has been sold. Yes, it's very emotionally difficult for me to do this, but as a family, my kids and I know it's the right thing to do. The hull has been in our family since 1980; she was launched in 1988; we enjoyed two offshore trips to Mexico, returning on the first one via Hawaii and Alaska, sailing over 30,000 nautical miles. She was our one and only home for a total of 13 years and those were the best years of my life. However, without Peter, it's no longer fun or easy. I've spent the last four years supervising transport back to Canada from Mexico, surviving a fire at sea and subsequently overseeing a complete electrical rewiring job and other major maintenance, and spending thousands of dollars on moorage for a boat that sits at the dock looking sad and lonely.
>
> However, I have a lifetime of memories that are priceless to me. I just want what is best for the boat, and to move on with my life. I thoroughly enjoy helping others achieve their dreams of sailing offshore, and I'm doing that as Commodore of BCA. I work hard at maintaining contact with my cruising friends through emails and phone calls, writing articles for *Currents* (BCA's monthly newsletter), hosting potluck parties for returning cruisers, and taking advantage of opportunities to crew for others. Travel will always be a big part of my life. In that regard, I'll always have the wanderlust... (Email July 14, 2009)

To Believe

Ever since the day Peter died, I struggled with deep spiritual questions. I wanted to believe, *really believe*, that I would see him again in heaven, that we would be together again one day. I didn't want to be told. I didn't want a scientific, logical explanation. I just wanted to believe this with all my heart.

I had been taught as a child that those who ask for forgiveness and follow Christ will go to heaven when they die. I learned this in childhood in a number of churches; Pentecostal, Anglican, United, and the Alliance Church, when my parents made several moves as my Dad searched for a way to earn a living. In each church, they sent me off to Sunday School and I was "saved" when I was 13; though I don't think I understood what that really meant at the time. As an adult, I attended and sang in the choir of a Catholic church for three years – but that was mostly because of the beautiful music created by a very talented music director. He recruited Peter to play the organ and me to join the choir. We felt very welcome there and made many friends within the choir.

When Peter and I were in high school together, we regularly attended church on Sundays and morning prayer meetings at school, as part of the Inter-School Christian Fellowship to which we both belonged. Peter was president of this school club. When he was about 17, he told me he wanted to become a United Church minister. However, due to his aptitude and talents, his high school counsellors wisely directed him towards engineering and to the Regular Officers' Training Plan offered by the RCAF, that would pay his way through university.

When we went on to university together, we joined Inter-Varsity Christian Fellowship, but something horrible happened at one of the first meetings that changed our lives and our religious beliefs forever – well...almost forever. We discovered that other more senior students were radical academics who spent most of the meetings debating which was the *real true* church of God – Catholic, United? Anglican? Peter and I were so shaken and shocked that we didn't know what to believe. We were only 18, naive, easily influenced by our peers and confused. It wasn't until many years later that we could finally talk about this experience with each other

116

objectively. That's no excuse, but it *is* the reality of what happened. We not only walked out of that meeting, we walked out of "church" or organized religion, for the rest of our married life.

However, New Beginnings Community Church in Surrey, BC, which my daughter and her family attended, was non-judgemental, casual, patient and fun. After Peter's death I started going to Sunday services on a regular basis with my family, grateful for how caring the congregation had been and enjoying the down-to-earth sermons by Pastor Ian and the great music provided by the talented worship teams. I asked questions of Ian and some of the elders, went on several women's spiritual retreats, and I started attending and sometimes hosting a Ladies Bible Study group. I actually read the Bible cover to cover in 90 days through a program offered by New Beginnings Community Church, complete with study guide, a video and discussion groups once a week. It was within this caring community of believers that I began to see church and religion in a totally different light than I ever had before.

I've already recounted some events during which I've felt Peter's presence. I had one more really significant spiritual experience. On the evening of December 9, 2008, I was taking great care in getting dressed as it was a very special night for me. It was the BCA Annual General Meeting, at which the members would be voting on a new slate of officers and I had been nominated for Commodore. As I surveyed jewellery appropriate for the occasion, I decided to wear my wedding rings, which I had stopped wearing nearly a year earlier. I was recalling what an outstanding, respected Commodore Peter had been, and how much I had learned standing by his side. I felt grateful. As I slipped the rings on my finger, I said a quick prayer that he would be present to see me follow in his footsteps by accepting this incredible new honour and privilege tonight.

That evening I was indeed elected Commodore and I received wonderful supportive comments from many members, congratulating me and assuring me that they knew I'd do a good job. It was most heart warming. However, before the evening was over, Don Brown gave his closing comments as the outgoing Commodore, and he started to tell a story that he had told me previously. I knew what it was as soon as he began, and gave close friends at my table a signal that I was probably going to cry. Well, somehow I managed not to cry, but many of them had tears in their eyes. Here, in Don's own words, is that wonderful story:

In early 2005, I experienced one of those moments that are magical and mysterious, leaving you wondering what just happened and what does it mean? I was in my second year as the Speakers Watchkeeper in Vancouver and was leaving a meeting in the lounge at Spruce Harbour Marina. On my way out, I was playing Alfonse and Gaston (a bumbling pair of Frenchmen with a penchant for politeness) at the door with Peter Doherty who had, along with Glenora, just attended the same meeting. I had seen Peter in passing but we had not been introduced, nor had I had an opportunity to speak with him. After coming down the stairs from the second-floor lounge to the dock, we stopped and spoke for a minute or two and Peter passed on a great joke that he said that I should feel free to use as he had "been dining out on it for years". Just two guys chatting on the dock in the dark. We bade each other good night, then we headed off in opposite directions.

I was struck that something special but intangible had passed between us. I turned, as if to speak, but just caught a glimpse of Peter with his Tilley hat and packsack walking down the dock and disappearing into the fog. I never saw Peter again. He passed away suddenly a short time later, but I will never forget that moment and the image is indelibly etched on my memory. The unspoken message I was left with that evening was recognition of the value of service, acknowledgement of intention, encouragement to continue and participate, the offer of resources and the extension of a hand in friendship. The belief in the value of what our organization offers to the sailing community could hardly have been more powerfully communicated. It was pretty clear to me that the BCA was a cause I was prepared to continue to support. When the opportunity arose to serve as Commodore, the decision was a relatively easy one. It has been a hugely rewarding experience. Thank you Peter, for the inspiration. (Don Brown, December 9, 2008)

Hearing Don's story, I suddenly knew why I'd worn Peter's rings that night. He was there. I felt his presence encouraging me, supporting me. Every person in the room who had known him remembered his incredible leadership within BCA and realized that that was why Don had served as Commodore. And I realized that was why I was going to be the next Commodore.

However, it wasn't just Peter who inspired and enabled me to run for Commodore. It was God. When Peter died, I had all the usual questions, "Where is he?" "Will I ever see him again?" I didn't blame God for taking him away, but I begged Him in my prayers to give me some answers. I was sure there must be a reason I had been left alone. I reasoned that perhaps God had his own plan for *me*. Thus began a voyage of a very different kind than the offshore voyages Peter and I shared together. It has been a journey to find the meaning of Peter's death and of my own life. Today, I can say I believe I've found it.

The following is part of my testimony (my story of my journey back to my Christian faith) that I gave to the congregation of New Beginnings Community Church on the occasion of my baptism on June 13, 2010.

In retrospect, I can see that it was actually Peter's death that triggered my return to faith and to church. You see, without him, I didn't know who I was or where I was going. I didn't know for sure where Peter had gone either. Was he in heaven? Were my memories of him all that were left? Or was he just a pile of ashes? I had always thought I believed in heaven and life everlasting, but when I lost the person I loved most, there was so much more at stake for me. I began to doubt my beliefs and I started asking questions.

My search for understanding led to chats with church members, joining a grief therapy group, sessions with a Christian counsellor, reading many books – including the Bible – and a lot of time in silent prayer. My constant prayer during that troubled time was, 'Dear Heavenly Father, please give me courage, guidance and strength.' I was pleading with God to show me the silver lining in all the dreams that had been shattered for me.

And...God delivered in spades! In the last five years, he has opened doors for me to so many new opportunities, new friends, new adventures and new joys that I never even previously imagined could happen to me. Just recently in my Bible readings, I came across a scripture Tara had highlighted for me years ago that expresses this so well:

> *For I am going to do something in your days, that you would not believe, even if you were told.*
> (Habakkuk 1:5)

It's true, if someone had told me even five or six years ago that I'd skipper our 50-foot sailboat across the Sea of Cortes, that I'd be living in a basement suite in Surrey, that I'd learn how to swim and snorkel at age 62, that I'd travel to New Caledonia, Australia and South America, that I'd be taking piano lessons and singing in a show chorus, that I'd be elected Commodore of BCA - I would never have believed it. It's only because of God's guidance, and the strength and courage He's given me that these things have been possible. Yes, He had a plan for me. Even more unbelievable five or six years ago is that I would be attending church regularly, reading the Bible and praying every day, serving in ministry and as a church administrator—and being baptised! What a joyous journey it's been!

It was through Sunday morning services and messages, women's retreats with Debbie, ladies Bible studies, Alpha, social gatherings and friendships, and now reading the Bible cover to cover in 90 days, that I started to finally understand what was meant by a personal relationship with Christ and the need for fellowship within a community of believers. I now believe that "church" is the worldwide community of those who believe in Christ and the salvation He offers. It's Christ's kingdom. It's certainly not a building or even a name. More specifically, I realize now that I needed the fellowship of a Christian community in which to grow and to learn that -- and I did that, right here at New Beginnings.

Being baptised is a big commitment and for me an important milestone in my life. It ranks right up there with the day I graduated, got married, gave birth to my first child, or made my first offshore passage. Although I made my decision to accept Christ over 50 years ago, I don't think I really understood what that meant...at that time. In the last five years, I've been seeking answers, and getting them, and steadily growing in my faith and in my love for God. Today I know that I'm doing the right thing to be baptised—it's what Jesus commanded us to do. I know I still have a lot to learn, but the journey I start today will be an even richer one because Christ will be walking beside me. Who knows what the Lord has yet in store for me? I'm ready...

I was immensely comforted by the fact that God was the one who was always there for me. I learned you can pray aloud or silently, with eyes open or eyes closed. He is always there. Even when I struggle to find the words to pray, I know that God knows my heart and understands what I need without even saying the words.

However, I also learned that God is more likely to speak to me if I'm still and calm, just listening for Him.

I don't mean I've actually heard His voice talking to me, although there are those who have, but it was the soft persistent nudges, a voice inside of me telling me what I should do and knowing that a decision I had made was right. Some people refer to this as having a gut instinct that something is true or right. God speaks to us in many ways: through His word (the Bible), song lyrics, persistent thoughts and nudges, music, and for me through nature—the warmth of the sun, the sound of soft rain on the roof, the beauty of a sunset, and the power and majesty of the ocean.

Many times in my life, I have known without any doubt that what I was doing was the right thing, that what was happening was meant to be. The first time I recall this happening was on my wedding day. I was a bundle of nerves, experiencing typical bridal jitters, fussing about details, and worrying that everything would go well. After my father walked me down the aisle and I stood beside Peter, one of our high school classmates, who was a good friend, sang *Ave Maria*. She sang it beautifully. My heart slowed down. My hands and knees stopped shaking. My breathing became more normal. And as I looked up into Peter's eyes, a sense of calm descended and everything else around me in the church disappeared except Peter, God and the beautiful music. At that moment, I knew with full certainty and without a doubt that what I was doing at that moment in time was right and good and that it was meant to be.

Today I can say with the same conviction that I am where I am meant to be, that what I am doing is the right thing and that it's part of God's plan for me. That feeling, that God had another plan for me, came as a fleeting thought on the day Peter died; but it's only in the last couple of years that I've known and felt it with full certainty. Today I understand that Peter's death was actually the trigger or the catalyst that brought me back to faith. For this I am truly grateful.

Today...I believe.

Who am I?

I've already written about my shock at realizing I was a widow. Yes, I am no longer a wife. However, I am a mother, grandmother, sister, daughter, aunt, cousin, friend and neighbour. I am retired, but that doesn't mean I don't have jobs. In addition to writing this book and studying music, I work as a volunteer for three non-profit organizations: New Beginnings Community Church, Bluewater Cruising Association, and the Maple Leaf Singers. And I am developing other new interests. As a result I could add to the list: administrator, past commodore, secretary, pianist, singer, writer, gardener in training, dog and cat lover, enthusiastic hostess and cook. And as you read this book, I have now become a published author!

I could add "sailor", because I will always be a sailor at heart, but I don't do much of that anymore. First of all, I no longer have a boat. Secondly, I have had osteoarthritis issues that make it difficult for me to balance and move quickly, both of which are essential for safety on a sailboat. The final reason is because I'm just too busy finding and enjoying new dreams.

Most important of all, I am a child of God. I walk with Him every day. I'm never alone.

The Spiritual Gifts Evaluation that my counsellor, Irene Flett, did with me was a good starting point to discover my talents: hospitality, administration and leadership. But the opportunities that have come to me in the past six years have also given me new insights and knowledge that I didn't have before. So many of the comments I have received from friends, starting with all the sympathy cards and condolence notes, mentioned my strength. One friend told me it was my strength that made it possible for Peter to do all the things he did in his lifetime. I really never thought of myself as being a strong person, but when I think of everything I've gone through, I believe it now. God gave me the gift of strength and courage when I needed it most.

My gift of hospitality has encouraged me to host dinners and parties to celebrate family special occasions, to get offshore cruisers together, and to provide a venue for church seminars, Bluewater gatherings, and author's circle meetings. I like nothing better than having a bunch of people come to my home to eat, drink, share stories and learn from each other.

My administrative skills were honed during years of public service, and today I serve as the volunteer part-time administrator for New Beginnings Community Church and Secretary for the Maple Leaf Singers. I enjoy writing newsletters, collecting information from members and compiling it, and doing everything as efficiently as possible. It's the same joy I get completing a very difficult Sudoku puzzle in record time. I've worked out a routine and a strategy for that, just as I have for other administrative activities. I've always loved keeping track of things—the family budget, address lists of friends, reconciling a bank statement, to do lists, and keeping a journal.

And finally, the gift of leadership gave me an opportunity to enjoy the honour and privilege of leading a 1,000-member offshore sailing club for two years. The election as Commodore of BCA was more than an achievement to me; it was a joy to be serving my bluewater family. I love what the Association does and I believe in it. It's an association of Dreamers (dreaming about sailing offshore), Doers (those out there doing it – sailing offshore) and Doners (those who have done it and have returned from their voyage). The Dreamers learn as they attend monthly club nights, read the newsletter, attend education courses and fleet programs. The Doers write letters from offshore that appear in the monthly newsletter, to inspire the Dreamers. And the Doners come home to become mentors and most likely will do a presentation at a Club Night about their trip and what they learned. Peter and I did all those things. Then we came back and started dreaming about going again, a second time. What a joy to have led an organization that supports activities that allow dreamers to realize their dreams.

During the time that I served as Commodore I learned many significant things about myself I never knew and probably would never have found out if Peter were still alive. I know he'd be proud of me, of course. Without him, I doubt I would ever have travelled from my home town, completed a university degree, changed careers as often and as successfully as I did or travelled the world. His encouragement was always there.

"Shoot for the moon. Even if you miss, you'll land among the stars."
(Brian Littrel)

One thing I learned a lot about was public speaking. I was incredibly nervous at the first club night I chaired in January 2009. My good friend Sally Holland told me afterwards that I talked so fast, she could barely understand what I was saying – I always talk fast when I'm excited or enthusiastic about something. In December 2010, when I gave my well-paced final report to the membership at the annual general meeting and received a standing ovation, Sally pointed out to me how far I'd come!

I've always enjoyed sharing whatever I learned. During my career in the federal government, I was often told I was a team player. I liked working with people, compiling their thoughts and ideas into a policy manual. I enjoyed teaching too, whether high school math (which is how I started my career at age 21), business courses to middle-aged women re-entering the work force, pre-school activities for toddlers, or effective writing courses for employees.

Some of the many things that give me so much enjoyment today are things I would not have been doing if Peter were still alive. For example, I realized that I'd always loved music but my own involvement had been limited by our constant moves over the years and overshadowed by my husband's incredible piano talent. Ever since I was a child, I'd wanted to take piano lessons, but my parents couldn't afford it and once I married Peter, he was so happy to play for me that I didn't need to learn myself! As a teenager, I did take voice lessons and I sang in my church choir, school glee club and the University of Alberta Mixed Chorus. I've always enjoyed choral music, but that wasn't a practical hobby I could pursue while ocean cruising. Now that I do have the opportunity to learn more about music, I'm enjoying it immensely.

I know with absolute certainty, that if Peter were still alive today, none of these things would have happened. We'd still be out there sailing together on the oceans of the world on *Wanderlust V* and loving it. In all honesty, I have to say I'd give up everything to be back out there beside him; that's where I'd rather be, *but...*

I give thanks to the Lord every night for my blessings. God is good!

Steps to Survival – Stage 6

❖ Save the most difficult decisions until later, until you really feel ready to deal with them.
❖ Consider your health in making decisions.
❖ *Believe* that God can do miraculous things.
❖ Seek help and advice from trusted professionals.
❖ Don't question visitations or feeling the presence of your loved one. Enjoy it. You don't have to justify to anyone what you feel.
❖ Listen, really listen, to hear God speak to you.
❖ Make a list of who you are—mother, daughter, secretary, soccer coach, golfer, etc.
❖ If you don't know what your spiritual gifts are, find out!
❖ Shoot for the moon!

7

The Seventh Wave

"...Let the pain and the sorrow
Be washed away
In the waves of his mercy..."
(©1998 Vineyard Songs, adapted from Psalm 42)

Surfers and sailors have long contended the existence of the phenomenon known as the "Seventh Wave" even though it's been denounced as poppycock by scientists. According to the lore, if a surfer or boater counts the incoming waves of a set, the seventh wave is the one to catch for the ultimate ride. If you catch it right, it will propel your dinghy off the beach and into deep water where you can safely lower your outboard or dig in your oars. Surfers also consider the seventh wave to be the "big one" or the ultimate ride. Rather than suffering waves of grief, I feel certain I am now riding the seventh wave; a wave of mercy, celebrating the end of the grief process.

Of course, reaching the seventh stage of grief has not come easily - or quickly. It has taken me seven years to complete my voyage through grief, seven years since my beloved Peter was taken from me. Sometimes the months have seemed like years and, as I've written in this book, the voyage has been challenging, frightening, even overwhelming. But here I am completing this book in the seventh year since Peter's death. I can truly say that I am happy again, that my life has purpose and meaning and that every day I am grateful to God to be alive. What a voyage!

The Number Seven

To me, it is not at all surprising that it is the seventh year after Peter's death that I am completing the seventh stage of grief. The number seven has always had special significance to me. Whenever I've been in a game where someone asked me to pick a number between one and ten, I've always picked seven – it's my favourite number. For many people, seven is considered a lucky number. Seven conjures up only good or positive things like seventh heaven, the Seven Wonders of the World, the seven dwarfs, the seven chakra (parts of the body), and the Group of Seven (Canadian artists). The ancient astronomers interpreted the seven visible celestial bodies as

> **Stage 7 of Grief – Acceptance & Hope:** During this, the last of the seven stages in this grief model, you learn to accept and deal with the reality of your situation. Acceptance does not necessarily mean instant happiness. Given the pain and turmoil you have experienced, you can never return to the carefree, untroubled *you* that existed before this tragedy. But you will find a way forward.

deities influencing and controlling every aspect of their lives. Also, something I just recently realized in studying piano is that there are seven notes in the musical scale - A B C D E F G. All other pitches are variations of these notes. Man named these notes, but it was God who created the sounds and the variations which I enjoy so much today, singing or playing the piano.

Finally, the number seven is God's divine or holy number. From the seven days of creation to the seven seals of Revelation, scripture is saturated with the number seven or numbers that are multiples of seven, such as 14 or 70. One example is that God created the earth in seven days, and rested on the last day, the Sabbath. So should we. Rest is essential to recovering from grief.

The Ten Commandments Moses received were the very first version of the written Word of God, and are located in the 70th chapter of the Bible (Exodus 20). The Bible mentions 14 times that they were written on tablets of stone. The Ten Commandments are good rules for anyone about how to live well and at peace, during and after you've completed your voyage through grief.

Numerous times in the Bible it took seven days or seven times to complete a task:

- It took God seven days to create the earth.

- God waited seven days for Noah to get all the animals aboard the Ark.
- Noah waited seven days for the dove to return.
- Israel marched around the city of Jericho seven times before taking control of it.
- Solomon was seven years in building the temple.

For more examples of God's holy number 7, see www.biblewheel.com/topics/seven.asp or www.angelfire.com/az/rainbowbridge/seven.html or read Michael Hoggard's book, *By Divine Order*.

Looking Back

After Peter died I never thought that one day I'd be able to look back and to reflect on his death and the many changes it has made to my life and that of my family. At that time, the shock, the pain, the uncertainty were all too great. But today I am able to reflect without going to pieces and to admit that I do have some heartfelt regrets about what will never be. The greatest is that my three youngest grandchildren will never know their Poppa. They will never have Peter as their friend, mentor or role model.

Another regret is that none of my five grandchildren will ever really know the cruising life we knew and loved aboard *Wanderlust V*. Our own two children, Ryan and Tara, had grown up with her, and Peter and I had enjoyed teaching sailing to our first two grandchildren, T'ea and Matthew, for four summers from 1999 to 2002, when they were between the ages of four and eight. However, they will never stand a night watch on *Wanderlust V*, or drop a bottle into the ocean halfway to a destination from her deck. Ryan's little ones, Angie, Daryan and Trea, will probably hardly even remember that they ever went sailing on *Wanderlust V* when they were toddlers. But...perhaps there'll be another sailboat in my family sometime in the years to come.

My own personal regret is that I didn't get to French Polynesia with Peter on *Wanderlust V*. That had always been my number one dream destination. I've seen many pictures of Hiva Oa taken by other cruisers, and I always said, "That's *so* beautiful. I've got to go there and see that myself!" I *will* get there yet - it's number one on my bucket list – but it won't be aboard *Wanderlust V*, unfortunately.

There is one sober realization or confession I feel compelled to make, looking back, because there may be other people also suffering grief who have felt the same thing. In my third stage of grief, as I described in Chapter 3, I asked, "Who can I blame for Peter's death?" At that point, I couldn't blame anyone. But today I know one person I can blame. This admission is something I've wrestled with for the past year. It's been hard to declare publicly, but here goes - *I now realize I can blame Peter himself for dying.*

No, he didn't want to die and, no, he didn't consciously prepare for it, but...he'd smoked off and on all his life. He loved to overindulge in rich and fatty food, and he wasn't ever active in sports or physical fitness even as a young man. Furthermore, he spent most of his life overweight. If he'd taken better care of himself, he might have lived longer.

I seriously disapprove of smoking, and he knew it, so he did it behind my back. I made the discovery in 2001 and spent a whole night tossing, turning and debating, but in the morning, I confronted him. With tears streaming down my face, I told him, "I love you so much that I just want us to be together always, to grow old together. If you're going to kill yourself with cigarettes, we may as well go our separate ways right now. And somehow we'll figure out how to divide this boat down the middle!" It was the first and only time in our marriage I ever threatened to divorce him, but it was tough love - and it worked! That day he stopped smoking, really stopped, and as the days went on, not smoking became a cause and a goal he became passionate about, like so many other goals he had in life.

Peter only had one request. He wanted me to verbally ask him every day, "Did you have a cigarette today?" He knew he couldn't look into my eyes and lie to my face, and knowing that I would ask him that question at the end of each day was the key to keeping him honest and helping him to totally and finally kick the habit. In addition, when he was diagnosed in 2002 with raging diabetes (normal blood sugar reading is 6.5; his was 22) just months before we were due to leave for offshore, he totally changed his eating and exercising habits, and lost 60 pounds. This also improved his overall health.

Peter lived life to the fullest; he enjoyed treats and having fun. In fact, we both took a small penalty on our pensions to retire early, because we both believed in enjoying life while we were still able. What's the point of living to be 100 if you aren't enjoying it?

Therefore, I forgive him. After all, forgiveness is what love is all about.

Our family doctor told me after this death that the steps Peter took to stop smoking and to lose weight probably added an three extra years to his life — the period from 2002, when we retired and left for offshore, until his death in 2005. I will be forever grateful to Peter and to God for giving me those three wonderful years which we spent together 24/7, doing what we loved most — being together on *Wanderlust V*.

The Present

Although my life has totally changed and will never be the same again, I have done my mourning and I can now look back at a lifetime of happy memories. Right now I'm riding the seventh wave - a wave of joy - enjoying my new life and many new dreams. That doesn't mean that I *never* cry when I think of Peter. Another cruising friend who lost her husband and remarried, told me candidly, shortly after Peter's death, that there isn't a day in her life that she doesn't think of her first husband, if only for a moment.

I think of Peter every day, and sometimes I cry and once in a while I sob. I shed many tears as I was writing this book. But I have accepted that he is gone, that I have a good life and that I have new dreams that bring me joy.

About a year ago, I bought my own home, a two-bedroom bungalow in a gated community in Surrey, BC, about a 15-minute drive from my daughter's family and a 25-minute drive from my son and his family. I love the house and the neighbourhood! In hindsight, I wish I'd done this sooner – but I just wasn't ready to do it sooner. After Peter's death, living alone was scary and intimidating. I needed the emotional and physical support of my family. They had lost their Dad and Poppa, and they needed me.

There is a right time for everything. There was a right time to sell the boat. And six years after Peter's death was the right time for me to start living alone.

Today, I enjoy the freedom to make my own decisions, but admit I've made some bad ones. I've wasted money on things I didn't really need or want and I didn't manage my investments well the year I bought the house, which resulted in a huge tax assessment and having one of my pensions cut back. But small decisions are wonderful—eating what I like, getting up when I want, decorating and furnishing my home the way I like it and having complete control over the TV remote. I enjoy being in charge of my own life. That may have something to do with the fact that I was an only child. I grew up alone without brothers or sisters competing with me or telling me what to do.

Having a slightly larger home has given me more opportunity to entertain and to host friends for dinner or overnight stays. In the first ten months after I moved in, I hosted five large celebration parties with 15 to 30 guests. I've also started doing a bit of gardening, which I haven't done in 30 years (pretty difficult on a boat!). My complex has a professional gardener who comes in once a week to mow and rake the lawns, and trim shrubs as needed. However, I have a flower bed at the front of my house, where I put in colorful bedding plants last spring and planted bulbs in the fall. In a strip of soil along the south side of my house, I've grown tomatoes, lettuce and other vegetables, as well as tall and fragrant sweet peas and beautiful dahlias. At the back, I have a small fenced patio, which gives me space for some patio furniture and a BBQ, lots of potted plants and flower boxes. My dog Tilley likes it too, as I can let her out freely on the patio, whereas everywhere else in the complex, she has to be on a leash.

My only regret is that it does not have a view of the water. I miss being near or looking out at the water. I miss sleeping on a boat that rocks gently in the water. But if I lived near the water I wouldn't be close to my family, nor could I afford it. Life is full of compromises. And although my house is perfect for me as a single person and for many of the other couples who live here, I doubt this house would have ever worked for Peter and me together. There's no workshop, not enough space for two desks and two computers without forgoing the guest room, and there's only a single car garage.

This is the first time in my life I've ever lived alone. When I left home to attend university, I boarded with a family and had a roommate. Then I married Peter immediately after graduation. I knew I couldn't live alone on the boat in Vancouver; it was hard enough for one month in La Paz while waiting for the Dockwise ship to arrive. But just as I've discovered I enjoy gardening, I've also discovered that I really like living alone, especially as a retired person.

Even though I live alone, I'm not lonely. I have many friends who I invite coffee, dinner or parties. I enjoy hosting meetings and seminars in my home and I encourage out-of-town guests to stay with me when they visit Vancouver. I'm involved in so many activities that I'm usually out somewhere every day or evening — meetings, chorus rehearsals, piano lessons, church services, shopping, taking two or three walks a day with Tilley, visiting family, having my family join me on Sundays for dinner, and joining my neighbours in our club house for coffee on Saturday mornings or playing cards on Tuesday evenings.

My house has also been a quiet, peaceful and healthy place that has allowed me to reflect - and to write this book! My desk looks out over a beautiful common green area. My best time for writing is late at night. I'm not bothering anyone if I'm up until 2 am at the computer and I'm free to sleep in the next morning if I wish. The only thing that might wake me is the gardener mowing the lawn on Friday mornings at 9 am!

Happy Moments

I mentioned my first "happy moment" after Peter's death was seeing my new grandson Daryan for the first time. There were many that followed but the most significant ones were:

- singing Christmas carols while I exercised in the pool and felt the warm sun shining directly on my face in 2005;
- snorkelling in tropical waters in 2006;
- cruising around South America in 2007;

- performing my first big show with the Maple Leaf Singers in 2008 (it gave me goose bumps!);
- serving as Commodore of BCA from 2009 to 2010; and
- being baptised in June 2010.

The most recent happy "event" is that I have accomplished the long-time dream of writing a book – this one! I am now a published author. It's been an exciting year for me, and the beginning of what I hope will be a new career as an author and speaker, with other books to follow.

Finally, my beloved *Wanderlust V* also has had a happy ending. She was first sold to a couple in June 2009, who absolutely loved her. They had been living aboard a smaller sailboat for a few years and wanted something larger in which to eventually head offshore. My family and I thought we'd found the perfect new owners and home for *Wanderlust V*. Soon afterwards, her new owners took her out for a week of sailing in the Gulf Islands and sent me beautiful pictures of her under sail and at anchor. But this was not to be *Wanderlust V*'s happy ending. Sometimes happy endings come in stages, with ups and downs in between.

Two weeks later after receiving the sailing photos, we learned that the couple had suddenly separated (not for any reason relating to the boat, apparently) and that *Wanderlust V* was up for sale once more. It took another eight months before she was sold; this time to Andy Cain, an Australian and an experienced sailor, who really loves her and is taking good care of her. My family and I had a visit aboard with him at the False Creek Yacht Club in Vancouver in early March 2011. I was impressed with the offshore preparations he'd made.

On March 24, 2011, *Wanderlust V* sailed proudly out of English Bay, flying the Australian flag. She is now officially registered in Sydney, Australia, and that's her destination. Take a look at Andy's website, www.wanderlustv.weebly.com (Wanderlust V – The Pacific Adventure) to see his route, photos, blog and more. I've been enjoying following the *further* adventures of *Wanderlust V*, and I hope to stay in contact with Andy and his future ocean passages.

Yes, I still shed a few tears knowing she is gone and that I may never see her again. But I am also absolutely thrilled that she was heading back out to blue water. That's what she was built to do.

Final Thoughts

Throughout this long voyage of grief, one hurting step at a time, I have searched for meaning in my grief. Writing this book has been the final step. It has certainly been more therapeutic than anything else I've done in the last six years. It has made me think hard about what I've lost and the blessings I've gained. Through Christ, I have begun to see that everything we have, everything we do, and everything we are is a gift. Even being a widow! I am at peace.

I won't say I wasn't lonely during my voyage of grief. I certainly was. And I still am sometimes. Every day there is something, however small, reminding me of Peter and I miss him so much. I grieved deeply for him. I grieved well, not seeking to avoid the challenges or pain. And I still grieve from time to time.

But I have found a peace that this world cannot give. It has come not by avoiding or removing the grief. It comes through the guidance, courage and strength I have received and continue to receive from God. His peace leads to acceptance, contentment, hope and new dreams.

For I have learned to be content whatever the circumstances...
I can do everything through Him who gives me strength.
(Philippians 4:10-13)

Final Steps to Survival

When you are ready, here's a list to get you started:

- ❖ Make a list of all the things you are grateful for.
- ❖ Make a "bucket list" of all the things you want to see and do before you die, and start doing them.
- ❖ What new understandings do you now have about your relationship with your loved one?
- ❖ Re-read your journal and reflect on how far you've come.
- ❖ Enjoy your freedoms. You are now in control. Make the most of your choices. You can even learn to take risks.
- ❖ Begin to look to the future. Experiment with new lifestyles, new ways of living each day. They might even turn out to be fun!
- ❖ Give yourself praise. Be compassionate to yourself. You are a richer, deeper, wiser person.
- ❖ *Celebrate Your Survival!*

Afterword

Although I've always wanted to write a book, I never dreamed about writing one about grief recovery. However, I have felt a real and immediate calling to write this book in order to pay forward all the support and help I received from the Surrey Hospice Society, New Beginnings Community Church, social workers, professional counsellors, doctors, friends and family.

It is my very great hope that sharing how I made it through to the other side of grief has helped you, the reader, to survive a similar loss or to help someone else who is grieving.

In this book, I have mentioned how God speaks and how there are moments in our lives that we know with full certainty that what we are doing is right and good, and meant to be. Writing this book also falls in that category.

God has continued to guide and help me write this book at every step along the way. Through friends of friends and just talking about what I am doing, I found a proofreader, people to review and provide endorsements, an editor, a publisher, and a web designer. It's almost been too easy – because God has simply placed all these people on my path in order to make this book happen.

Thank you to my friends, and thank you, dear God! I now know that I was meant to write this book, that it was part of God's plan for me.

Glenora Doherty
Surrey, British Columbia
7 March 2012

S/V Wanderlust V

Now.... watch for my next book! It's the book I always dreamed of writing. It will be a book about my many sailing adventures, both the joys and the challenges.

COMING SOON!
Wanderlust: 30,000 Nautical Miles in 30 Years

To be placed on my mailing list for updates and advance notice of publication, please go to my website and fill out the form on the "Contact" page:

W 5 • C O M M U N I C A T I O N S

www.w5communications.ca
OR
email me directly at glenora@w5communications.ca

About the Author:

Author, Writer & Speaker

Glenora Doherty, B.Ed., was born on a Saskatchewan farm, but grew up in Calgary, Alberta, where she married Peter Doherty, her high school sweetheart. She has lived in Germany, California, Mexico and five Canadian provinces. Her 35 year professional career included teaching and editing and she retired from the federal government as an Assistant Treaty Negotiator.

She has sailed over 30,000 nautical miles aboard the Reliance 44 ketch, Wanderlust V, which she and her family built from a bare hull, and has served as crew on other offshore boats. She is the Past Commodore of Bluewater Cruising Association; sings with Vancouver's fabulous show chorus, the Maple Leaf Singers; and volunteers as Administrator for New Beginnings Community Church.

She lives in her own home, 'Wanderer's Rest', in Surrey, BC, with her Havanese pup, Tilley, where she enjoys hosting family and friends. Her two married children and five grandchildren live nearby. She has published articles in Cruising World Magazine and Currents (the monthly newsletter of Bluewater Cruising Association). This is her first book.

Do you have an inspirational story with a message
and interested in becoming an Author of Influence?

Glenora Doherty is a graduate of the InspireABook program and a
member of the Inspired Authors Circle. If you want to get on the path
to be a published author by Influence Publishing or one of our imprints
please go to www.InspireABook.com

For information on the Authors circle and other Authors of Influence
please go to www.InspiredAuthorsCircle.com

Each month a new book title is released that "Inspires Higher
Knowledge" Each pre-launch campaign is supported by the other
Authors of Influence with Free E-Books, Audio Books, Mp3's and
other gifts. For each book you purchase from the Influence Publishing
family you will receive $100's of Free gifts if you support our launches
by pre-ordering the books. Take a look at the gifts offered at:
www.SpiritualAuthorsCircle.com/book-launch-gifts/

Life Journey Publishing is an imprint of Influence Publishing.

More information on our other titles and how to submit your own
proposal can be found at www.InfluencePublishing.com

CPSIA information can be obtained at www.ICGtesting.com
Printed in the USA
LVOW070059090312

272244LV00004B/1/P